A huge thank you t
that mad

Without you there would be
no story to tell...

And an even bigger thank you
to the decent people
who helped me tell my story.

Cleo James

PART ONE

Secrets Kept

One

When was it, the first time he hit me?

Quite honestly I can't remember. I can recall the time he slammed the palm of his hand so hard into the side of my face that he dislocated my jaw. That wasn't the first time. I can recall the holiday in Devon when he shut my arm in the cottage door as I was trying to get away from him. We spent five hours in the A&E department getting my fractured wrist encased in plaster. That wasn't the first time. I can recall the night he squeezed his hands so tight around my throat that the next morning I sounded like Kathleen Turner after twenty Marlboros. That wasn't the first time. I can recall skin and muscle being squeezed just that bit too hard and spiteful pokes and supposedly playful pinches. But trying to pinpoint that first violation, the moment when I should have said to myself, 'Hang on a minute, this is not acceptable 'I can't quite place it. Keeping all things equal I can't recall the first time I hit him either.

It is with complete clarity however that I recall the first time I laid eyes on him. You can really only "click" with another person if the feeling is mutual and if those feelings are very strong rarely will human nature let us walk away. If both parties are free to embark on a relationship it can be the start of something beautiful. When it happens between two people who are not free to love another it can have dire consequences. Some of us are too weak to resist. We are too greedy and inquisitive to leave it be. Sometimes too miserable in our current situation to resist the lure of excitement and passion. Others find it hard to resist regardless of their happiness status. There are countless reasons why we veer off a familiar path, steering our lives in a different direction.

Back then my life was on track. I enjoyed my job as a nurse (for the most part). That alone was enough to be grateful for. I once administered chemotherapy to a patient who had just been diagnosed with cancer. I was surprised at how upbeat he seemed.

'You're doing so well 'I commented as I searched for a vein for the cannula to be inserted.

'Well, I've been signed off work for eight weeks 'he said jovially. 'Every cloud has a silver lining.'

My close circle of friends were as important to me as I was to them. They made up for the fact that I had no family to speak of. The twenty-five-year-old man who impregnated a fifteen year old girl one drunken night in November 1967 declined to stay around and witness the consequences of his actions. Nine months later in August 1968 that girl became my mother. Her family overcome with shame and disapproval refused to have any contact with either of us. My mother had a very powerful "sod em" attitude back then that failed to wane over the years. I never once heard her bemoan the fact that she had been left alone and all credit goes to her for giving me a loving and stable albeit unconventional childhood. Leaving me with kindly neighbours on the council estate in South West London where we lived she earned money doing an assortment of unskilled low paid jobs. By scrimping and scrapping and long hard graft she managed to put herself through university gaining a law degree and eventually practising as a solicitor. She died aged forty eight following a short illness but not before she had forged a reasonably successful career. I was thirty three when she passed away. With no other family to consider she left everything to me including her three bedroom flat in a mansion block off the Fulham Road at the Chelsea end. I worked in the local hospital and friends lived nearby, so apart from the obvious sadness at my mothers passing, life was really quite good.

A day shift in A&E in February 2002 was to change all that. I took the folder handed to me by my colleague. The first thing that caught my eye was the yellow post it note stuck to the top of the page. We stuck those on to indicate good looking male patients. With a wink at her I made my way to the cubicle and pulled back the curtain.

I was expecting something nice. What I saw took my breath away. Dark hair with an olive complexion, stubble surrounding plump lips and a strong jawline. We locked eyes and neither wanted to be the first to look away. It was only as my eyes travelled down his handsome face over the broad shoulders did I realise he was holding his left arm up resting it on his chest. His hand was wrapped in what appeared to be a very dirty item of clothing.
I looked down at the name on his notes. Mark Palmer.

'Hello Mark, I'm Cleo '(my mother had listened to jazz since she was eight - Cleo Laine was my namesake).

His face broke into the sweetest smile as he spoke.

'Hi Cleo, have you come to ease my pain?'

'I'll do my best 'I said laughing at the cheesy question.

'Okay, what's happened here then? 'I said reaching for his hand.

He was staring at me so intently I was having trouble focusing. I needed to get on with my job. Concentrate Cleo, concentrate I silently admonished myself.

He was a builder and had been carrying a steel on his shoulder, tripping up on a loose floorboard putting his arms out to break his fall. The steel slid from his shoulder landing on his left hand. My initial observation after removing the crude bandage was very disappointing, though not from a medical point of view. On his finger was a wedding ring. Damn, why did I feel so deflated? I carried out a few perfunctory tests, telling him he would need an X-ray to determine any broken or fractured bones.

'We'll get the pain under control for now but unfortunately we'll have to cut off your wedding ring as your fingers are starting to swell.'

'Don't worry about it. Wish it had never been put there in the first place.'

I wasn't quite sure how to respond to that. I needed to clean his hand up and put a temporary dressing on. God I was making a meal of it. My colleagues must have been cursing me wondering why I was taking so long. It was so unlike me. It was quite simple, I did not want to let him go. As I gently wiped away the dried up blood I could feel his eyes boring into me.

'Are you married Cleo?'

I kept my head down concentrating on his wounds.

'No, I'm not the marrying type 'I answered honestly.

'Do you fancy meeting for a drink sometime?'

I looked up then, so desperate to say yes, knowing I couldn't, but not quite able to say no either. As it happened I didn't get the chance to say anything. There was an almighty crash and several voices shouting at once followed by cries for help from Lucy the student nurse. It was a case of all hands to the pump. Excusing myself I darted up the corridor to find three nurses and our duty doctor attempting to hold down a man who appeared to be fitting. I grabbed a foot that was just about to connect with the doctors ribs. The situation was brought under control with the help of a little injection in the patient's backside. I was gone for no more than 10 minutes. Long enough for my yellow post it man to be seen to by another nurse who had arranged for him to go to x-ray. So that was it then. The first and last time I would encounter the beguiling Mark Palmer. An inexplicable feeling of emptiness washed over me at the thought. For the second time in an hour I silently admonished myself. Get a grip Cleo, get a bloody grip. He was an attractive guy, no more no less. Yet there was a connection there. I could feel it so strongly it was tangible. There was little doubt in my mind that the feeling was mutual.

My shift came to an end shortly afterwards and as I walked home I made a mental list in my head of jobs that needed doing indoors and in which order of priority. I had only lived in my flat for six months so I was still in the process of putting my stamp on it. Hand embossed fabric covered the walls in my bedroom as opposed to wallpaper. I had made my own headboard, a huge cut of MDF and a layer of thick foam covered in grey velvet with brass studs banged in around the edges. I had a carpenter in to lay wooden floors in the living areas but for the bedroom I had chosen a cream coloured carpet with such a deep pile that you lost sight of the edges of your feet when you walked on it. It was sumptuous and decadent and I loved it. An image suddenly came to my mind of Mark Palmer lying naked on my bed. Or should I say how I thought he might look naked. The more I tried to dispel the image the more vivid it became. Think kitchen units, think light fittings, think paint samples I told myself.

Think anything but bloody Mark Palmer.

Two

I slept badly that night, tossing and turning, checking the clock, debating whether to get up and make a camomile tea or lay there and hope that sleep would creep up on me. The day had unsettled me or to be more precise meeting Mark had unsettled me. How ironic to look back and realise that he had the power to cause me sleepless nights before he even had my phone number. I was a mess at work the next day. There are some jobs that allow you to go to work not feeling one hundred percent. Being a nurse in a casualty dept on a Saturday is not one of them. The weather had been particularly bad for the last couple of weeks. Heavy rain followed by dramatic drops in temperature. Perfect conditions for icy roads and pavements, which in turn became perfect conditions for traffic accidents and people slipping over and breaking bones. I was coming to the end of my shift, treating my second broken arm of the day when Lucy the student nurse popped her head into the cubicle.

'Looks like you've got an admirer. Stunning bunch of flowers have just arrived for you at reception.'

I knew instinctively they were from Mark and the thought had me grinning from ear to ear.

I finished with my patient and practically skipped to reception to retrieve my flowers. And what a bunch they were. More in keeping with a hotel lobby than a home, the smell had already permeated the reception area and had nearly eradicated the usual aroma of bodily fluids and alcohol.

‘Ohhh aren't you a lucky girl ’sighed Joan the receptionist.‘ I didn't know you were seeing anyone, do tell all.’

‘Nothing to tell you at the moment Joan ’I said laughing ‘but I promise as soon as I have anything to report you'll be the first to know.’

I opened the small card attached to the cellophane. Two words written on it.

Heal Me xxx

Had I not been so excited at the thought of Mark sending me flowers I would have given more thought to how odd those words were.

The huge bouquet was rather heavy and I wondered if I would have to get the bus home. It was only a fifteen minute walk but it was raining and I didn't want them to get ruined.

The choice was taken out of my hands. As I left the building heading towards the main road I heard my name being called. I turned to see Mark leaning on the wall next to the entrance, arm in a sling with a nicely bandaged hand. Our smiles when we saw each other were mirror images.

‘You got them then ’he said indicating the flowers with a tilt of his head.

‘Thank you, they’re really beautiful.’

‘No, it should me be thanking you for the way you looked after me yesterday ’he protested.

Apparently he had gone straight from x-ray to the operating theatre to have a pin inserted in his middle finger. ‘It could have been much worse according to the doctor.’

‘You’ve been lucky then ’I replied.

‘In more ways than one ’he said as he reached up his good

hand and touched my face. It felt more intimate than a kiss and my stomach flipped.

'Why? 'I asked.

'Because I've met you Cleo.'

Oh God, it was simultaneously corny yet wonderful.

I had been on the receiving end of all sorts of chat up lines over the years, some of which had led to dates, a few that had led to relationships, but I had never experienced such intense feelings about a man in such a short space of time.

We were sheltered somewhat from the rain but it really wasn't an evening to be outside. Everyone around us was moving briskly, umbrellas held close to them for fear of the wind turning the nylon inside out and rendering them useless.

'Shall we go for a drink, maybe something to eat? 'he suggested.

'And what am I supposed to do with half of Nine Elms flower market between my arms?'

'You can put them in the nearest bin for all I care, as long as you come with me.'

Despite my misgivings I couldn't help myself. How weak was I to continue that evening knowing full well he was married. I took the flowers back to Joan without having to offer up an explanation. She was too busy dealing with a woman who had seen an alien in her room the night before and wanted an examination to see if he had interfered with her while she was asleep.

As I walked back to Mark, I knew that whether it be in a pub or in a restaurant, or on the street for that matter, I had to explain that as much as I wanted to, I could not embark on a clandestine relationship. It was simple. I would explain I didn't get involved with married men, he would walk away and we would feel gutted for a few days afterwards knowing that in another place in another time things could have been different. I was not expecting him to tell me he had already left his wife.

As the rain was so heavy I suggested a pizza place a short walk away more for its location than the quality of the food. Even so, by the time we sat down at a table in the window we were wiping raindrops off of our faces with our napkins. He ordered a bottle of wine and we clinked glasses before our first sip. As they touched I said 'cheers 'at the same time he said 'to us'.

'Look Mark 'hating that I had to say this. 'You're married and I really don't agree with affairs. I'm not going to deny I feel a connection with you but sadly some things are just not meant to be.'

'I've left her.'

I wasn't sure I heard him correctly.

'I've left her 'he repeated a bit louder.

I was speechless for a moment.

'For the night? 'I said stupidly.

'No Cleo, I mean I've left her as in it's over.'

An expression of confusion battled it out with an expression of happiness for a place on my face.

He continued. 'There are some things I need to tell you about me and I'm going to be as honest as I can so will you just listen and ask questions afterwards?'

I nodded my head in agreement.

'I'm not going to tell you my wife doesn't understand me ' he started. 'I don't want her to understand me. I don't want anything from her. She's my second wife by the way 'he added as an after thought.

I knew his date of birth. I had seen it on his notes in AE yesterday. It was in August, the day before mine although I was five years younger. He was only thirty eight and had been married twice. That did not bode well. He went on to give me a potted history beginning with the twenty-fifth year of his life. A big white wedding to a neurotic anorexic followed nine months later by a baby boy they named Harry. By the age of twenty seven it was all over bar the shouting and divorce proceedings were instigated. A move away from the area to live in Scotland for two years to play semi-pro rugby had ended in disaster. A particularly nasty tackle left him with a knee injury that prevented him playing his beloved game. With nowhere better to go he headed back to his hometown of London. Moving back in with his parents who lived in Putney was a stop gap until he could find his own place. Out with his pals one night he met a woman in a pub. One thing led to another and before he knew it he had moved into her flat in Notting Hill. Eighteen months later he bought an engagement ring from a stall in Portobello Road market and proposed to her while on holiday in Dubai. She began planning the wedding of the century which was the last thing he wanted. In the end they had flown to New York on Concorde (she worked for British Airways) and were married in City Hall by a registrar who he said reminded him of Margarita Pracatan from the Clive James show.

He'd hardly come up for air since the start of his story but I had managed to sink a glass of wine and was relieved when he noticed and poured me another.

Just over a year into the marriage history repeated itself. He met a woman in a pub while out with his mates, somehow forgetting that his wife was waiting indoors for him. She was a Swedish woman visiting London with friends. Following an exchange of numbers he was able to arrange trips to her home town of Stockholm without his wife even knowing he had been anywhere. His wife's work with British Airways involved travel, so when she went away he made the most of it. It was supposed to be a bit of fun to break the monotony of life. However it ended up being very unfunny when she told him she was pregnant and she was keeping it.

At this point I couldn't stop myself. 'Fuck, you have got to be kidding me? 'I said rather more loudly than I had intended.

'I only wish I was 'he said softly.

'Even when you told her you were married? 'I said incredulous at the thought of having a baby with another woman's husband.

For the first time he hesitated.

He hesitated for quite a while. Long enough for me to guess what was coming next.

'You didn't tell her you were married 'I said stating a fact rather than asking a question. He nodded in agreement. He did tell her however that he didn't want more kids. He wanted her to have an abortion but his words fell on deaf ears and she went ahead with the pregnancy. They stayed in contact by phone with Mark visiting Sweden when wifey's rota allowed.

She gave birth to a son and when I interrupted asking how old he was Mark looked somewhat vague. 'Er, I'm not sure exactly how old but he's toddling about and he's got teeth'.

I asked how he could deny his parents a relationship with their grandson. He brushed it off lightly. 'How could I tell them? To all intents and purposes I was married and trying for a baby with my wife.'

How ironic that his parents were waiting for a grandchild from their daughter-in-law when they already had a grandson they knew nothing about.

'And what did you tell the Swedish woman?'

'Oh, I just told her that I didn't get on with my parents and wasn't in contact with them.'

I was searching for the shame in his face, maybe a look of regret. But no, nothing, nada, sweet FA.

'I don't want anything to do with her or the kid anymore ' he declared. 'I think it's best to leave them to get on with their own lives and let me get on with mine.'

I interpreted that to mean I'm bailing out.

'Cleo', he said reaching for my hand. 'I am one fucked up

man. I've been unhappy as far back as I can remember.'

And at that moment he looked so vulnerable. I wanted to hold him in my arms and reassure him that everything was going to work out in the end.

I could never have envisaged the horrendous journey it would take to get there. Looking back would I have changed any of it? With my hand on my heart I can honestly say most of it.

Three

Over the course of the next few weeks Mark gradually moved himself and his belongings into my flat. I had a key cut for him so he could come and go as he pleased.

Despite his bandaged hand we were all over each other and when I wasn't at work most of our time was spent in bed. His body was better than I had imagined it would be. He told me if he could have created an ideal woman she would look exactly like me. He told me I was beautiful and perfect and he would love me forever. I knew he had received some rather upsetting phone calls from his soon to be ex-wife. I did not blame her for calling. It's how most women would react when their husband announces out of the blue that he's leaving.

She'd picked him up from the hospital the day after his accident. In the car on the way home he had told her he was unhappy and the marriage wasn't working out. She had told him not to be stupid and blamed it on the anaesthetic still in his system. He assured her he was of sound mind and it was at that point she'd nearly lost control of the car and just missed veering into a cyclist driving round Shepherds Bush Green. Back home, he said, she begged him to reconsider, literally begged by getting down on her knees and clinging onto him. He tried to prise her off but she was inconsolable and buried her face in his legs sobbing all the while. In the end he had to drag her along the hallway and shake her off at the front door in a bid to escape. I would not have wished such feelings of desperation on my worst enemy. My mind would not rest on the imagination front and I tortured myself with images of a woman I had never even met left discarded like those old shoes you see on the roadside. He had asked his father to go round and collect his stuff and take it all back to the family home which I thought was rather a cowardly request. When I questioned Mark as to the reason he wouldn't go himself his answer was simple.' I never go back Cleo.'

He had taken time off work due to the injury to his hand but as it was his own building company, his team were carrying on with the renovations and he was still earning. We could not bear to be apart from each other. Mark often met me for lunch, breaking up his day if I was working a long shift. One particular day I was leaving the hospital to grab a sandwich with a colleague, Jeremy, a doctor who I had been working with earlier that morning. We were discussing a patients unusual symptoms when I noticed Mark sitting outside the coffee shop. I excused myself, saying goodbye to Jeremy and rushed over. I was so happy to see him but by the look on his face the feeling was far from mutual. As I bent down to kiss him he pulled his face away and I ended up kissing his neck.

'What's the matter? 'I asked puzzled by his reaction.

His face, which up until that moment had only ever been handsome was contorted as if in pain.

'What's wrong? 'I asked again.

'Who was that you were talking to? 'he asked, ignoring my questions.

'A doctor I work with 'I answered with a slight note of indignation. I wasn't waiting to hear anymore on the subject. 'I'm getting a sandwich, do you want anything?'

He shook his head and I joined the queue. As I checked the board for the fillings I could not help but feel a very slight niggle beginning to form. I did not do jealousy and neither did I wish to be the object of someone else's jealous thoughts. I decided to let it go and hope it was a blip in our otherwise perfect relationship.

Mark's hand healed successfully and he was soon back to

business. My shift pattern at work was four days on/three days off. How I cherished those days off. They would generally be during the week so Mark would leave early for work. I would either go for a run in the park just over Battersea bridge or grab my swimming kit and head for the baths where my mum had taught me how to swim when I was four. I'd head home maybe stopping off at the supermarket if I needed some shopping or popping into the overpriced but worth it Italian delicatessen round the corner. Then back to the flat for some therapy which is what housework and cleaning were to me. I have always craved neatness and order. My mum told me when I was little I used to line my dolls up in order of their hair length.

My favourite time of the day though was when Mark would call to tell me he was on his way home. I'd have a bottle of wine chilling or breathing depending on the colour, dinner would be under way and I would run him a bath with his favourite bath salts. In those early days most nights I'd end up in the bath with him. It was a huge claw footed cast iron affair that we both fitted into comfortably. No mean feat considering Mark was six foot one and I was five foot ten.

We had some of our deepest chats during those long soaks, alcohol relaxing our minds and our tongues. I was getting the impression that his upbringing was perhaps lacking in love. He spoke of his childhood without self-pity and very matter of fact. His parents obviously lived by the adage 'Spare the rod and spoil the child'.

He recalled episodes of strict discipline from both parents though in my mind they sounded more like violent outbursts. My mother had never laid a finger on me so I found it quite difficult to listen to. He tried to justify their behaviour by admitting that he was an 'utter nightmare 'growing up. Mark laughed as if he was proud of being a pain and deserved to be punished. I thought it was far from funny and told him so.

'I don't agree with hitting kids, or adults for that matter.

I couldn't even step on a spider.'

'Well that's because you Cleo, are a genuinely sweet and kind person 'he said rubbing his hands up and down my legs that were either side of him. 'So kind in fact that you are going to do some lovely things to me before we leave this bathroom.'

A couple of nights later I answered the home phone to my dearest friend Lisa. She was arranging a night out for a group of friends for her upcoming birthday.

'You have got to come, we always celebrate our birthdays together and I haven't seen you in ages, please please say you'll come.'

I had known Lisa all my life. Her lovely mum and dad Patsy and Ron were the next door neighbours who looked after me when my mum was working all hours. Lisa was married with a two year old daughter and a four year old son so nights out for her were few and far between. She was right, we hadn't seen each other in ages. Come to think of it I'd seen hardly anybody but Mark since early February. I knew I had been fobbing friends off who had called to meet up for a drink or catch a film. Didn't that always happen at the beginning of a new relationship I asked myself. Surely it wore off and life would naturally return to a semblance of normality. We spoke about her plans to meet up in our local pub then head up to Covent Garden for cocktails and a boogie.

'And don't forget Cleo darling, dress to impress.'

'Oh I intend to 'I said as we ended the call.

Mark had been pacing in and out of the bedroom during my conversation with Lisa. I had been watching him from my position lying on the bed. It was the only room in the flat with a home phone in it. Not that I minded him eavesdropping, there was nothing to hide, but I wondered aloud what he was actually doing.

He came at me so suddenly that for a second I froze. It

wasn't actually me he was aiming at I realised, it was the phone sitting on the bedside table. Even so I rolled off the bed just to be on the safe side (literally). He pulled his arm back and smashed his fist into it while I looked on in horror from my crouched position on the opposite side of the bed. Again and again he sent his fist crashing into the now cracked and broken phone. It lasted no more than a few seconds before he wore himself out with the force of his punches. I didn't move. I couldn't move. I watched as he sank down bypassing the bed sliding down to the floor. He dropped his head into his hands and just sat there.

I desperately wanted to scream at him. What the hell did he think he was doing? Had he lost his mind? What on earth made him do it?

I asked none of these questions. Instead I stared at the back of his head and wondered what the hell was going on inside it. Eventually we had to move ourselves. I cleaned up his bloody hand for the second time in two months in the bathroom where we had recently shared such loving moments. I asked him then what had just happened.

'When I heard you making arrangements to go out I got angry, and when I heard you say 'I intend to 'I lost it. I'm so so sorry. I'll replace the phone. I love you so much.'

The very slight niggle that had began to form in the coffee shop not so long ago took on real shape that evening. I would have been a complete fool not to see that Mark was jealous beyond reason.

'You got angry because I was going out and you heard me say I intend to 'I reiterated. 'Do you realise how crazy that sounds? Let me tell you 'I continued, 'I can go out whenever I want, wherever I want, with whoever I want. I don't though because the majority of the time I chose to be with you. I trust you implicitly and I expect that to be reciprocated.'

Mark shrugged his shoulders and shook his head while

repeating over again 'I'm sorry, I'm sorry, I'm sorry'.

If I was hoping for a more in-depth explanation for his violent outburst I was to be left feeling disappointed. Sitting on the edge of the bath he took my face in his hands and pulled it towards him. He kissed me so gently and with such tenderness, it was hard to believe that half an hour earlier he was so full of anger. After cleaning Mark up I started on the bedroom. I managed to get the drops of blood out of the carpet which was something to be grateful for at least. I unplugged the phone from the socket in the wall and threw it in the bin. The handset had multi coloured wires hanging out where the plastic had been cracked open. It was beyond repair but it would have been binned regardless. I wanted no reminder of that awful night which was ironic considering the most significant reminder was sitting in an armchair in my living room nursing a glass of wine.

Lying in bed later that night with Mark snoring gently beside me I was able to go through every detail in my head without interruption.

Whichever way I thought about it, the facts remained the same. He had serious anger issues. The question was, what was he going to do about it?

Four

The answer was nothing. He came home from work the following day with cling film wrapped around the top of his arm to protect a tattoo he'd had done earlier that day. As he removed it I saw the symbol at the bottom and guessed what he had done. I had an interest in all things oriental and had gone to evening classes to learn Chinese before I had met Mark. It was an incredibly difficult language to understand and I only lasted one term. I did however learn how to write my name which was now etched in bold blue ink down his arm. I suppose my reaction should have involved an element of fawning but I couldn't bring myself to perform. I was not impressed but decided to keep my thoughts to myself.

'Now you'll always be with me 'he whispered pulling me in close to him.

I wasn't sure if the shiver I felt going down my spine was due to his warm breath on my neck or the ominous tone to his words. Despite the upset brought on by my arrangements to celebrate Lisa's birthday I was determined to go out. If I gave in to Mark at this stage I would be giving him the impression that I found his behaviour acceptable.

I was also genuinely looking forward to seeing the girls. Mark and I had isolated ourselves from everyone since we had met. Harry, the thirteen-year-old son from his first marriage, called often attempting to make arrangements to see his Dad. Mark refused to communicate with Harry's mother so it was left to a young boy who was desperate to see his Dad and a man who wasn't really that bothered. It made me very uncomfortable to hear Mark making excuses. I would have preferred feeble ones as opposed to the convoluted stories that he came out with.

'Sorry son, can't see you today, gotta go and sort out a boiler that's blown up in the house I'm working on. They've had to evacuate the street in case there's a gas leak.'

I had met his parents who appeared to be very nice. In fact a little too nice. I expected them to have some degree of allegiance to their second daughter in law, after all she had been part of their family for a number of years, taking holidays together, celebrating Christmas's and birthdays.

But no, not a bit of it. No mention of her, forgotten it seemed in the blink of an eye, while I was welcomed into the family with open arms.

I was off work on that Friday and decided to dedicate the whole day to myself in preparation for the night ahead. I had an appointment at the hairdressers for hi-lites and the beauty salon for a bikini wax. The day started with a cup of tea placed on my bedside table and a kiss placed on my forehead.

'Morning darling' Mark spoke gently brushing my hair out of my face.

I smiled in answer. His outburst had been a few days earlier and he had been particularly loving and attentive since.

'I was thinking 'he said, 'how about we try that Thai place tonight, the one we passed the other day. It looked busy didn't it?'

'Oh Mark, I would have loved to but you know I'm out with the girls tonight 'I said as casually as I could. 'Remember, it's Lisa's birthday.'

If I'd have blinked at that exact moment I would have missed it. The anger that flashed across his features, the fire in his eyes. But I didn't blink and I knew he was not happy.

'Oh yeah, so what time will you be home? 'he questioned as he stood up.

The change in his mood was so obvious and uncalled for that it was on the tip of my tongue to say 'Saturday afternoon'.

Before I had a chance to answer he cut in telling me he might as well go out with the boys from work anyway as it was Friday.

'Well, we're both sorted then aren't we 'I said with a wink trying to lighten the mood.

He left the flat slamming the front door behind him which was no mean feat. It had a soft closure mechanism and you really had to give it a tug to make that noise. I actually spoke out loud to myself 'What the hell was that about?'.

With nobody to give me any clues I came to my own conclusion. Mark was a fucked up individual and I was getting ready to party. By six o'clock that evening I was manicured, pedicured, hi-lighted, blowdried, waxed, tweezed and debating. Jeans, leather jacket, high heel boots or figure hugging dress, jean jacket, high heel shoes? I laid both outfits out on the bed then selected the appropriate underwear for each one. I put on a CD of old skool classics, turned up the volume and poured myself a glass of wine. I danced naked around the bedroom first in my boots then in my shoes to see which pair were the most comfortable. It was about halfway through Candi Staton singing about young hearts running free that I got a feeling I wasn't alone. I turned the music right down and listened carefully. The sound of footsteps on the wooden floor coming towards the bedroom had my heart beating ten to the dozen.

'Is that you Mark? 'I called out tentatively. Silence followed adding to my fear.

He had definitely said he was going out straight from work. Had I left the front door on the latch when I took the rubbish down earlier on and forgotten to take it off? Was there a mad man with a knife in my hallway?

With my heart threatening to burst out of my chest I moved cautiously towards the bedroom door which was slightly ajar. Should I slam it shut or open it fully? My legs wobbled in fear, not helped by the four inch heels I was wearing. There wouldn't be a struggle to get my clothes off if it was a rapist standing on the other side of the door. I was naked from the ankles up. I lunged at the door falling against it and heard a familiar voice shouting my name.

'Cleo, it's me you nutcase, you nearly broke my nose.'

The relief of hearing Mark's voice sent me into hysterical laughter. I could detect a chuckle in his voice as he asked if it was safe to come in. I threw myself on the bed rolling around getting tangled up in my clothes. Mark joined me and we laughed till tears rolled down our cheeks and our stomachs hurt. As we calmed down the mood changed and a sexual charge took over. In the space of fifteen minutes I had experienced relaxation, excitement, extreme fear, extreme relief, hysterical happiness culminating in explosive sex.

Afterwards I lay my head on his chest while he ran his fingers through my hair.

'Don't go out Cleo, stay with me 'he said softly.

I could feel his warm breath on my head and I knew this gentle loving atmosphere could change in a second if I didn't give in to his request. I won't lie and say I battled with myself. It was a no-brainer. I reached for my mobile and called Lisa apologising that I wouldn't be able to make it due to a bout of sickness that had started earlier that day. The excuse sounded as feeble to my own ears as it did to her's. With promises to make it up to her I ended the call with a pang of guilt that I had let my friend down.

And so we continued living our insular life together, interrupted occasionally by a visit to see Mark's parents in Putney, or taking them out for Sunday lunch. His brother John lived with Kerry and they had two young boys. Considering I wasn't a lover of babies or young children I found Callum and Kurt rather endearing and was happy to spend time with them in their cramped and somewhat chaotic household.

Potentially life could have been perfect. Unfortunately

Mark made that impossible. His mood swings and erratic behaviour were hard to handle and even more frustrating was the fact that there did not appear to be any rhyme or reason as to what set him off.

One minute we would be cuddling up on the sofa declaring how much we loved each other. I'd leave the room to put the kettle on and come back to find him sitting there fists clenched and a face like thunder. Walking through a minefield would have been less treacherous than walking hand in hand down the road with him. If a man happened to glance in my direction Mark's hand would tighten around mine just to let me know he'd clocked it. As if I had any control over who looked at me. He would bump into people on purpose leaving me to apologise. When crossing the road he would ignore the pedestrian crossings and chose a totally inappropriate spot to get to the other side of the road, dragging me with him as we dodged the traffic. If a driver dared to beep his horn Mark would give them a volley of abuse threatening all manner of violent ends. It seemed as though he antagonised the simplest of situations looking for any excuse to blow his top.

My hair which was very long had to be worn in a bun at work for obvious reasons so on my days off I often wore it in a loose plait that hung down my back. Mark got into the habit of pulling on it whenever he stood behind me. Sometimes just a little too hard for my liking. He done it once in the queue in Sainsbury's and I stamped so hard on his foot in retaliation that he cried out in pain. Of course I said it was an accident and apologised but I was uncomfortable with the fact that his actions were causing reactions from me that up until then had never been in my nature. There were pokes and jabs from his iron like fingers especially in my ribs which was particularly painful as there wasn't much fat round my middle. If our relationship was to be censored by the film industry we would come under the category of mild violence.

A bit slap stick and no serious intention to cause pain. If I ever told Mark he was hurting me he would laugh and say 'I'm only joking, did I hurt you, oh I'm sorry Baby'.

His behaviour was puzzling. The usual suspects could not be blamed. He did drink alcohol but there was certainly no abuse of it. An occasional glass of wine at home, a pint of Guinness if we went to the pub. I knew he had taken cocaine in the past but who hadn't. It was London and the once rich man's drug had become the poor man's choice. He had a good reputation as a builder and there were no financial worries. Without anything to work on it became increasingly difficult to put up with the moodiness.

Eventually I did get my night out with the girls. Only this time I couldn't be bothered to beautify myself. Quite frankly I didn't have the energy. Dealing with Mark was exhausting and if I was in any doubt about the negative effect he was having on me my friends soon confirmed it.

'Bloody Hell, you look rough 'was one of the first comments that greeted me as I walked through the door of the pub where my lovely girls were waiting for me. The fact that I had come straight from work did not help. Normally I would not dream of going out without going home and showering the shit of the day down the plughole. I knew if I had gone home to Mark there would have been the Spanish inquisition before I even got to the bathroom. So there I sat flanked on either side by dear friends and a glass of wine on the table in front of me waiting to be sipped. They looked and smelt gorgeous while scrub trousers and a faded old grey sweatshirt with my hair pulled back in a messy bun completed my look. Lisa stood up and started the first words of our usual toast.

'To those'...........she gave us a moment to join in, and then we all carried on rather loudly 'of us who wish us well, those who don't can go to hell.'

The smell of antiseptic wafted up my nostrils as I lifted the glass to my mouth and took a large gulp.

'So Rapunzel', said Lisa as she came to sit next to me planting a kiss on my cheek.

'Why Rapunzel? 'I said pointing to my bun 'no plait.'

'I'm referring to you being locked in a tower unable to escape rather than your hairstyle.'

Without warning my eyes filled with tears that threatened to spill down my face.

'I knew it 'she said clenching her fists in anger. 'I said to Mum, there's something not right there with our Cleo and that bloke.'

There was no stopping the spillage of tears when I heard Lisa say 'our Cleo'. I had been missing my mum so much lately. She would have sussed Mark out in an instant. I could see her in my minds eye.' Cleo, the man has sociopathic, psychopathic, narcissistic tendencies. Leave him immediately.'

Lisa and her parents were the nearest thing I had to family and I knew if I needed their support they would be there for me. She pleaded with me to go to Patsy's the following Sunday for one of her mum's famous roast dinners so we could talk about what was going on. I hugged and thanked her and said I would try to make it. I left the pub not long after that with promises to see everybody soon. I wasn't in the mood to be sociable, however I was in the mood to tell Mark that I wanted him to move out.

Easier thought than done. Thankful for the Dutch courage the two large glasses of wine had given me, I practised my speech as I walked home. I let myself into the flat to find him lying on the sofa wearing just a pair of boxer shorts, impossibly handsome, hair damp from the shower, skin scrubbed clean, the smell of him in the air. When he saw me his face lit up as if I was the most wondrous thing he had ever seen.

'You're home Darling', he said jumping up from the sofa coming towards me with his arms open. 'I thought your shift ended at eleven.'

I had told him I was working late to save the inevitable mood swing it would cause if I had told the truth about going out. But I'd fucked up. It was just before ten and he would smell alcohol on my breath.

Sure enough, the questioning started as soon as he had kissed me full on the mouth.

'Have you been drinking?'

'Yes, I met up with the girls in the pub on the way home from work.'

'You never said.'

'No, you're right I didn't because of the fuss you would cause Mark.'

'So you think it's okay to lie to me 'his tone just verging on menacing.

'No, I don't, just like I don't think it's okay for you to mistreat me the way you do.'

'Mistreat you, mistreat you 'he repeated raising his voice. 'I absolutely adore you, how can you say that? 'he asked, flabbergasted at my accusation.

'You hardly let me out of your sight, you don't trust me. You accuse me of the most ridiculous things. You're aggressive and dangerous. You wear me out with your crazy moods and I don't think I can take it anymore.'

The sofa was the first item of furniture to be rearranged. Mark bent down and flipped it over roaring like an injured animal as he did so. It was like a scene from the Incredible Hulk after David Banner gets the hump and turns green. He was like a mad man grabbing hold of anything he could get his hands on and throwing it across the room. A side lamp whizzed past my face just missing my nose, several picture frames and a footstool ended up smashed lying in pieces on the wooden floor. It was extremely distressing to witness but there was no choice but to let him rage. Eventually after swiping the contents of the mantelpiece onto the marble hearth underneath he collapsed exhausted on the only clear area of floor space in the room. If he thought I was going to comfort him he would be in for a bloody long wait. While he was wallowing in his own self pity I grabbed a few essentials, clean uniform for work, underwear, toothbrush, jeans, a hoodie, swimming bag and phone charger.

'I want you and your gear out of here by tomorrow. Before you leave I want everything put back as it was, replace what you have smashed and repair what you have damaged. Put the keys back through the letterbox when you have finished.'

Without looking up he pleaded with me to help him.

'I can't Mark, you're beyond help.'

Five

I ran down the stairs and out onto the street. I couldn't drive as I'd had too much to drink. One guarantee of living in Chelsea was the steady stream of black cabs driving through the streets at all hours. I hailed one and ten minutes later I was pulling up outside the estate I had lived on until I left home at eighteen. The familiar smell of Zoflora disinfectant as I entered block C triggered memories of running up and down the concrete steps leading to three flats on every landing, little hands gliding along the black shiny iron banisters daring each other to jump from three steps, then four, then five until you found yourself at the top of the flight of twelve stairs. Many a sprained ankle had been tended to at the bottom of those steep steps following a misjudged landing or an over ambitious jump. I climbed the stairs to the third floor to number 9 and knocked as softly as I could bearing in mind the time was getting on. There is a cut off point for phone calls and door knocks. After nine o'clock at night there is a slight unease when you answer. You would never expect to see a policeman standing on your doorstep at three in the afternoon but it might enter your mind at midnight. Not wanting to scare Patsy, I pushed my hand in the letterbox and called her name as gently as I could.

'Pats it's me, Cleo, are you up?'

I waited then called again and then again a little louder. Looking through the small gap I heard movement and then my guardian angel came into view walking up the passage wrapped in her pink towelling dressing gown. Relief and emotion flooded through me and as Patsy opened the door I fell into her arms sobbing like a baby. Sitting at the kitchen table sipping a cup of hot sweet tea I gave her a blow by blow account of the events that had led me to seek refuge in the flat next door to my childhood home. She let me talk, snivel and cry all the way through my narrative until there was nothing left to say. She offered only comfort, the advice and opinions could wait until tomorrow she had said as she tucked me into the single bed in Lisa's old room.

Having spent all night either thinking or talking about Mark that despite what he had done I simply felt bereft. I had put my phone on silent on the short journey to Patsy's and hadn't looked at it since. My strong head instructed me to leave it be but my weak heart insisted I check it. Our hearts win out almost every time and this was no exception. Eighteen missed calls and seven texts. I knew it was vitally important not to read them. I could not be swayed by heartfelt apologies and declarations of love and empty promises.

With the phone in my hand I got out of bed and listened at the bedroom door before I carried on into the passage. I could hear the comforting snores of Ron and I was confident that Patsy was laying beside her beloved husband sound asleep herself. I opened the bin in the kitchen and pulled out a cardboard box that had previously contained six Bakewell tarts (no recycling back in 2002). Making sure my phone was turned off I placed it in the box. I opened the front door and put the latch on in case it shut behind me. On the landing in the corner was a rubbish chute. I knew from many years of emptying rubbish down it that the cast iron door creaked when you pulled it down and slammed shut loudly if you let it go too quickly. With great care I eased it open a fraction pushed the box through the gap and let it close as quietly as I had opened it.

If I was hoping for closure in hearing my only line of communication with Mark clanking down a rubbish chute I was sadly mistaken. After laying awake for what seemed like hours I finally managed to shut my brain down and give it some long overdue rest. That's not to say I slept like a baby but I did remain in bed till just gone seven the next morning which was late for me.

My first thought on waking was Mark. Where was he? How was he? What was he doing? My heart ached and my stomach churned. The smell of frying bacon that came wafting under the bedroom door would at any other time have left my mouth watering. That morning it made me feel nothing but nauseous. I made for the bathroom just in case.

'Are you alright in there love? 'Patsy enquired through the door.

'Give me a moment and I'll be with you 'I answered.

I splashed my face with cold water, catching sight of myself in the mirror above the sink wishing I hadn't. It was not pretty. How was it possible that a few weeks ago the man I was in love with was telling me I was the most beautiful woman he had ever met. If he saw me now he would retract his statement.

I had no idea why the sight of a man at a kitchen table tucking into a bacon sarnie would bring tears to my eyes but it did. It was a clear indication of how emotionally unstable I was.

'Ello my little cupcake 'Ron said as he got up and wrapped his big strong arms around me.' Come and sit down and tell me all about it.'

Fighting back tears and wiping my snotty nose I explained that I was all talked out but I had a favour to ask of him.

'Ask away my love.'

'If I make a list will you go to my flat and pick some things up, not much, just what I need for the next few days? 'I hesitated. 'Which leads me into asking the next favour.'

'Well I hope you're going to ask if you can stay here ' interrupted Patsy as she reached across the table and gripped my hand. 'And the answer to that is of course you bloody can.'

I went back to what was to be my bedroom for the next week or so to draw up a list for Ron. How ironic that Lisa and I played for hours in that very room with our pens and pencils writing lists with titles such as -

What I Want To Be When I Grow Up
What My Husband Will Look Like
Baby Boy Names
Baby Girl Names

I never imagined a list entitled

Possessions To Be Retrieved From My Flat Because My Psycho Boyfriend Has Driven Me Out

I desperately needed my address book. Having dumped my mobile I needed contact details of friends and work colleagues. I had decanted my Mum's ashes into an antique copper urn that sat on the windowsill so she could catch the sun and the light as they came through the glass. I promised her I would always keep her with me so the urn had to go on the list. I thought it best not to let Ron know what it contained just in case it made him nervous and he dropped it. My orchids didn't like being left on their own and they were used to me talking to them everyday. I had about five dotted around the flat and I couldn't bear the thought of them in full bloom with no-one there to appreciate their beauty.

My interest in all things oriental had spilled into my home furnishings and a Buddha in one form or another sat in every room. I was extremely upset when Mark knocked my favourite statue off of the mantelpiece the night before and I watched helplessly as it smashed onto the marble hearth. I had to have one with me so settled on the small Buddha head in the bathroom.

That day my shift was due to start at 11.00. I was in a dilemma. I hated to let work down but I would bet my life that Mark would go to the hospital to find me. My rota was in the kitchen drawer so he knew my days on and off. I couldn't risk it. I was safe if I stayed here. Isolated, helpless, miserable, heartbroken but safe. Without my mobile I had to use direct enquiries to get the number of the hospital. I called the main switchboard and asked to be put through to A&E.

'Good morning Accident and Emergency Department, how can I help you? 'Joan the receptionist answered.

'Joan, it's me, Cleo. Can you let whoever's in charge today know that I won't be in for the next few days.'

'Oh, are you alright love? Only I thought it strange when I saw your young man outside the hospital this morning. It wasn't even seven o'clock. I know because my shift started at seven this morning but I got in early to have my breakfast.'

Despite fully expecting him to turn up it still came as a shock to have it confirmed.

'Joan, I'm having some personal problems at the moment and without going into too much detail it would help me out if you could just say you haven't spoken to me if Mark happens to ask you anything about me. My phone is out of use and there is no other number I can be reached on.'

She assured me I could rely on her and looked up some colleagues phone numbers for me including my boss who I would have to call later that day to explain the complete mess I was in.

Ron went to my flat that afternoon to collect the items I had requested. I told him not to forget to pick up the keys that Mark had hopefully posted through the letterbox.

'Make sure he's not in there before you go in Ron, he's unstable and I don't want you getting hurt.'

'Don't you worry about me 'he said with a wink. 'I can look after myself.'

Patsy had informed Lisa of the situation and of course she came up to her Mum and Dad's to be with me. She had left the kids at home with their Dad and brought a box of wine with her instead.

Alcohol was the last thing I needed but the only thing I wanted and I did not possess the strength to deny myself.

By the time Ron returned I had sunk three glasses of wine and about four peanuts. My appetite had all but disappeared and requests from Lisa to eat something fell on deaf ears.

I'm not sure what I was expecting Ron to say he had found. Maybe that there had been a fire in the flat or that all the windows had been smashed in.

But no, nothing like that.

Apparently there had been no sign of anything untoward, not a thing out of place.

'In fact 'said Ron casting a disapproving glance round his own very lived in front room 'it looked like a bloody show home.'

Patsy gave him a playful tap round the head at the insinuation that their place was far from a show home.

'Got everything you asked for apart from the key. It was nowhere to be seen I'm afraid'.

First job tomorrow morning I thought to myself, get a locksmith.

Six

I had met Mark at the beginning of February and by the end of May my life was in chaos. Complete chaos. How could so much have happened in such a short space of time?

I felt like I had been on the longest rollercoaster ride in the world. I had stepped off the ride and now I needed stability. The carousel would suit me for a while. Sitting on a wooden horse going round in a circle. No jerky movements, no surprises.

I went seven days without seeing him. I doubt there was a single second in a minute in an hour that I did not think of him. On the morning of the eighth day I declared to Patsy and Ron that it was time for me to stop feeling sorry for myself. As lovely and kind as they were to me I needed my own space. Work had been equally understanding but I knew the pressure my colleagues were under when we were short staffed. Ron had arranged for the locks to be changed following his visit so with a set of shiny new keys in my pocket I headed back home. On the way I stopped off for the basics, bread, milk, cheese and wine. I still had the appetite of a sparrow so I didn't want to over do it and make myself feel sick. Cheese on toast was always a go to meal in times of stress.

Opening my front door and entering the hall felt unfamiliar. Despite Ron's reassurances I was convinced the flat would be in disarray. Thankfully I was wrong and it was like a show home just as Ron had said. Not a thing out of place. Every shard of broken glass had been swept up. Even the footstool had been repaired. The smashed frames had been replaced and hung back up on the wall. They were different from the previous ones but instantly I preferred them.

I went through to the bedroom and stood in front of the

mirrored wardrobes. So far there had been no sign of Mark in the flat. I had told him to take his stuff and go. My hand hovered over the handle and as I began to slide the door open I made a deal with myself. If his clothes were gone I would never see him ever again. I couldn't bear to look and shut my eyes tight. Two seconds later I opened my eyes to no gaps, no empty sections, hangers still with his shirts draping from them. I looked down and there were his Gucci loafers, with the wooden shoe trees keeping their shape. I loved those shoes on him. I knelt down and picked one up. Removing the tree I put my hand inside the shoe and brought it to my face. The gold buckle felt cold against my skin and the smell of leather caught the back of my throat. I imagined his bare foot stepping into the shoe and tears rolled down my face at the thought of never seeing him get dressed or undressed in this room again. I pulled my sweatshirt over my head and dropped it on the floor. I took his white linen shirt off its hanger and put it on, teaming it up with a tweed jacket with sleeves so long they covered my hands. Next I kicked off my trainers and socks and slid my feet into his loafers. Shuffling in the shoes that were four sizes too big for me I made my way to the bathroom where I opened the cabinet to find his toiletries still lined up in a neat row. I pulled up my sleeves and smeared a dollop of his moisturiser onto my face and began massaging it in with circular movements releasing the aroma. I closed my eyes imagining Mark's face close to mine breathing in the scent of him. I scooped a handful of his hair wax out of the tub and rubbed it over my hair. A light coating of dust had settled on his aftershaves that sat untouched on a glass shelf above the sink. I picked a random bottle and sprayed it into the air. I kept on spraying until I was choking in the perfumed mist and I staggered into the hallway to catch my breath. Just as my breathing was calming down and the coughing had eased up there was a knock at the door. A second later Mark's voice called my name through the letterbox. My heart soared and I was there in an instant, fingers greasy from the cream trying to turn the knob to let him in.

'Don't go Mark 'I shouted, 'I can't open the door. 'Even to myself I sounded hysterical. 'I can't open the fucking door.'

He made soothing noises through the letter box, calming me, instructing me to slow down and take deep breaths.

'I'm here Cleo, I'm here.'

There was no hiding the shocked expression on his face when he saw me.

'Oh God, what's going on? 'taking in the fact that I was wearing his clothes and looking like an extra from One Flew Over The Cuckoos Nest. Reaching out to pull me into his arms I answered with tears spilling down my cheeks.

'I don't know Mark, I haven't known what's going on from the moment I met you.'

Needless to say the inevitable happened. We spent the rest of that day in bed and in-between making love we talked, trying to sort out the mess we had created for ourselves. He told me he had spent the week back at his mum and dad's trying to sort his head out. He was extremely apologetic, wanting to take all the blame and I was quite happy to give it to him. He deserved it. I told him in no uncertain terms that if there was another episode of violence he would be out the door. Of course he assured me he would never actually hurt me. Smashing furniture up in a fit of rage was a release and he understood he needed to control his anger.

'I swear to you Cleo, it will never happen again.'

I let him believe I was taken in by his promises but for me it was a case of when it would happen again not if.

In those early days patterns were formed that were repeated countless times over the years. Following an outburst or upset Mark would buy extravagant gifts or book extortionate holidays to assuage his guilt. The day after our reunion he told me he was popping out to check on some work. Before leaving he must have told me he loved me about thirty times. He stared at me as I was eating toast and sipping my tea. He followed me to the bathroom and watched me clean my teeth. In the end I playfully told him to fuck off which he did returning a couple of hours later with a brochure for a stunning villa in Spain.

'That's ours for two weeks 'he said with a great big grin on his face.

'When? 'I asked trying to sound enthusiastic.

When he told me it was the last two weeks of June I couldn't help but voice my concerns. I was due back at work the following week and I didn't think I could get the leave at such short notice. Mark's answer was not to go back until after the holiday, that way they would still think I was off sick. Normally so conscientious I would not have dreamed of skiving off. How persuasive he was convincing me how lovely it would be to spend 24/7 with each other for two whole weeks. It should have been obvious to me how controlling Mark was as I agreed to his plan, making an appointment at the doctors to extend my sick certificate. My GP had signed me off with stress and told me to come back if I felt things weren't improving. I felt such a fraud sitting opposite the doctor lying through my teeth about how I was still struggling. She gave me a certificate for another four weeks.

With work sorted and me agreeing to the holiday Mark went into shopping overdrive insisting we buy new luggage that we didn't need and a whole new wardrobe of summer clothes each. I told him I was more than happy with my cut off Levis, a few vests and a couple of pairs of flip flops. Totally ignoring my protests he came home one evening after a shopping spree. There were bags of gear, including four pairs of Vilebrequin swimming trunks for himself and a bikini for me that cost enough to feed a small nation. It was also an example of the more you pay the less you get. The bikini top was so tiny it barely covered my nipples and the bottoms were the size of a Dairylea cheese spread triangle attached to some string.

He needn't have bothered wasting his money. Apart from going to the supermarket in our hire car twice in fourteen days in suitable attire we spent the rest of our time wandering around the isolated villa and its grounds completely naked. The brochure did not do it justice. I was expecting something special but on first sight it took my breath away. Set high in the Andalusian mountains it had come into view as we turned a sharp bend in the road and a slip road took us up a steep rugged path to reach the iron gated entrance. I remember feeling so safe and protected, confident in Mark's driving as he rested his hand on my leg in between gear changes. Inside the villa we discovered five bedrooms, three bathrooms, a kitchen bigger than my flat and a lounge with panoramic views over the mountains with the Mediterranean shimmering in the distance. As beautiful and stylish as it was inside, for me nothing could compare to the outside space which included a swimming pool so big a dolphin could have lived there quite happily. I asked why he had booked a villa of that size just for us. He explained that as it wasn't rented out for those two weeks the company had let him have it at a reduced rate. He didn't let on exactly what he paid but I had seen the price list in the brochure and normally it would have been rented for six thousands pounds per week in mid season. Before we left for Spain I had offered a contribution but he wouldn't hear of it. And so began two weeks of sheer uninterrupted bliss. The weather was perfect. Hot enough to have to dive in the pool to cool down but not so hot that we were sweating while relaxing on one of the several cabanas dotted around the pool area. We did the same thing everyday simply because the day before was so wonderful. We would have been depriving ourselves not to repeat it. Our days were filled with lovemaking, eating, drinking, swimming, talking, laughing and just being who we were. Or at least who I thought we were. I had been willingly and happily lulled into a sense of security that felt so good I didn't think to question anything. Mark was happy ergo I was happy. That was until the end of our holiday when we arrived at Malaga airport after dropping the hire car off.

As we made our way to the check-in desk a group of men fell into step behind us. They weren't particularly loud, just ribbing each other and laughing. I saw Mark glance back over his shoulder and within a nano second his whole demeanour had changed. I was pulling a bag on wheels with Mark walking the other side of it. He leaned towards me and put his arm around my back, his hand gripping my shoulder with a force I hadn't felt for a while. It was very awkward as the bag was between us and he was pulling me in closer to it. I'm sure he could feel the bag banging into my leg but he just kept propelling me forward walking far quicker than was necessary. There was still a way to go to the desk and I was just too uncomfortable to carry on in that position. Without thinking I pulled up abruptly intending to put the bag on the other side of me so Mark and I would be side by side. Unfortunately the man walking behind me hadn't realised that I had stopped and went into the back of me, stepping on the sole of my flip flop which prevented me moving forward. I lost my balance and fell forward onto my knees. He followed, landing on top of me which at least gave him a softer landing than the one I had.

'God, sorry about that, are you okay? 'he asked looking very concerned as he got himself back to a standing position, giving me his hand to help me up.

Before I had a chance to offer my apologies as it was clearly my fault Mark stepped up so close to the man's face that their noses were nigh on touching.

'Of course she's not alright you fucking arsehole.'

I scrambled to my feet feeling the tension in the air, hoping to diffuse the situation.

'Mark, it was my fault 'I explained grabbing his arm attempting to pull him away.

'Sorry mate 'the man said pulling away. 'It was an accident, I didn't see her stop.'

'No, you didn't see her stop cos you were too fucking busy looking at her arse 'Mark hissed at him.

The poor man looked petrified.

'No, no I wasn't honestly mate.'

Mark jabbed him hard in the chest.

'I'm not your fucking mate. Now do yourself a favour and fuck off you cunt.'

We still had two hours before we could board the plane and my nerves were in shreds worrying we were going to bump into the guy again. Mark hadn't got the anger out of his system and I could tell it was bubbling just under the surface keen to raise its ugly head or in Marks case ugly fists. My attempts to explain that it was actually my fault were met with sneers and snide remarks. He had his own theory about what had happened. He did agree it was my fault, though not for stopping. Where I had actually gone wrong according to him was wearing my denim cut offs in public. We were drinking beers at the bar when he said this and I nearly choked on my San Miguel when I realised he was deadly serious.

'So let me get this straight 'I asked incredulously. 'You are blaming me for your disproportionate anger towards another human being because in your paranoid mind he was checking out my arse which was fully covered by loose fitting denim?'

If any part of my body was being checked out I thought to

myself, it would have been my legs. I'd swam one hundred lengths everyday for the past two weeks and laid in the sun turning a lovely shade of golden brown with no white bits whatsoever. My legs were toned and tanned and if someone wanted to admire them, why not?

I asked him how he could spoil such a magical time by ending it with aggression and anger. He had the grace to look slightly shamefaced and sorry. Leaving me in the bar he returned a short while later with a duty free bag which he handed to me. In it was a pair of Prada sunglasses that I had tried on at Gatwick on our way out to Spain. A large bottle of my favourite perfume and a heavy silver bangle completed the guilt gift.

'For fucks sake Mark, you'll be broke if you carry on like this. Wouldn't it be easier on your bank balance and your brain to calm down and try and curb your aggression?'

He grabbed my hand and kissed it repeatedly.

'Forgive me, forgive my anger, I love you so much.'

I couldn't help but laugh at his craziness. He knew he had got away with it as he joined in with my laughter while removing the sunglasses from their box and putting them on me.

'Gorgeous, absolutely gorgeous 'he declared and with a gentle kiss on the tip of my nose all was forgotten.

Seven

The week before Mark walked into my life and smashed it to pieces I had gone for a drink with Marcia, a friend and colleague. It was utterly miserable on the weather front and was forecast to stay that way. We were in our local taking full advantage of happy hour which in our case should have been called miserable hour. We were fed up. Work had been hectic and we both felt in need of a break or at least something to look forward to.

'I need some sun on my bones 'I sighed checking out my pasty looking skin by pulling up the leg of my trousers revealing my shin to Marcia.

She nodded her head sadly. 'Girl, you not heard of fake tan? That leg is so white it's blinding me 'she said laughing and slapping her ample thigh.

'Well, it's alright for you with your year round caramel skin, you bitch 'I said with a smile on my face. She was of Jamaican descent and not only had she lucked out in the colour stakes, but she had been blessed with the shapeliest backside ever. We spoke about various holiday destinations and she mentioned she'd always wanted to go to Vegas.

'Let's do it 'I said.

I had been before and loved it. Tacky, vulgar, wild and fun. As we kissed and hugged our slightly tipsy goodbyes she promised me she would get to work on planning our trip. Two days later in the staff room at work she was asking me for a deposit to secure a seven night trip to Las Vegas staying at the Venetian leaving on October 13th.

Every molecule of my brain had been so consumed by Mark since the moment I had met him that I had completely forgotten about the Vegas shindig.

I was reminded of the trip by a message on the answerphone at home (the mobile phone that had been disposed of down the chute had never been replaced). It was Marcia.

'Hi Cleo, just getting things booked, Grand Canyon - by air or land? Call me asap. Viva Las Vegas.'

There followed a strange hur hur noise that may or may not have been her Elvis impersonation.

I laughed out loud, then it hit me. The thought of having to tell Mark I was going away for a week to one of the biggest party capitals of the world filled me with dread.

My next thought was to get a grip. I was going on holiday with my mate, not embarking on a career as a lap dancer.

Needless to say when the news was imparted to Mark later on that evening it went down like a burka at the playboy mansion.

Firstly I was accused of all sorts of behaviour ranging from a clandestine trip with a doctor from work (remember Jeremy?) to spending a week drinking, dancing and shagging my way through every nightclub on the strip. Secondly, I was put through the wringer regarding my holiday companion. Mark had not met Marcia yet and he started to convince himself that she didn't actually exist.

'Yeah, you're right Mark, this is all a conspiracy so I can travel five thousand miles to sleep with other men when I could actually do it within a two mile radius of here.'

'Why do you have to say things like that Cleo, the very thought makes me feel ill 'he growled through clenched teeth whilst banging his clenched fists against his thighs. He would have preferred them to be banging against my thighs I'm sure.

'Listen to me Mark, you can sit here winding yourself up all night but I need some sleep. I'm going to Las Vegas with or without your blessing so going on about it for the next few months will achieve absolutely fuck all. I love you very much and it would be really nice if you came to bed with me.'

I held my hand out to him. He took it and I led him to the

bedroom where we did what we always ended up doing.

Surprisingly Mark appeared to have heeded my words and he hardly mentioned my trip until about two weeks before I was due to go. Then he went into overdrive. He wanted to know the in's and out's of a duck's arse. I honestly did not have the answers. I was more than happy for Marcia to do all the arranging.

'I'll tell you what Mark 'I said to him one night about five days before we were due to go. 'I'll get Marcia to come round and she can show you the itinerary, that way you'll know exactly what is going on. Let me ring her now and tell her how interested you are.'

I knew full well that would embarrass Mark. He liked people to think that he was a nice easy going guy with perfect manners, not a bullying control freak.

'I just don't want you to go Babe's. I'm going to miss you so much.'

I reminded him we had spent seven days apart before and we had both survived.

Departure day arrived and I was battling to hide my excitement. Mark had been such a complete pain in the arse that I could not wait to get away from him. In the early hours of the morning before the alarm went off, he reached out for me and we made love. He kept repeating how much he loved me and kept asking me if I truly loved him. I dishonestly reassured him that I did.

Marcia had wanted me to meet her at her place so we could travel together in a cab to Heathrow but Mark had insisted on taking me all the way to the airport.

Before we left the flat he presented me with three envelopes numbered 1, 2 and 3. 'Open number one on the flight out, number two halfway through the week and number three on the flight home.'

As we approached the airport he got in the lane for the

short stay car park instead of the drop off passengers lane.

'Mark, just drop me off here, you don't have to come with me.

'Please let me 'he asked pitifully.

There was an embarrassing display of affection from Mark that would have been over the top if I had been going on a round the world trip for a year let alone a week in Vegas.

The sigh of relief that left my body as I waved him out of sight left me weak. I was free for seven days and seven nights. Free from questions, suspicion and accusations.

I opened envelope 1, five hours and four glasses of wine into the flight.

On the front of the card was a black and white picture of a rough sea, waves crashing to the shore with the words in bold:

I was just existing until I met you.

Inside there was not a space that did not have Mark's writing covering it. At first glance it looked like the writing of a madman. After reading a couple of lines I knew without a doubt that it was the writing of a madman.

Informing me his life would not be worth living if I wasn't in it was one thing but to go on reading that he would kill himself if I left him was quite another. I stopped reading by the fourth line.

When the flight attendant walked down the aisle with her trolley asking if anyone had any rubbish I handed her an empty packet of peanuts and three envelopes. One had been opened but two remained sealed never to see the light of day.

Still without a replacement mobile Mark had made sure to put Marcia's number in his phone. I had explained I would call to let him know I had arrived safely. He didn't even give my arse a chance to hit the seat in the limo that picked us up from the airport before he was calling Marcia. No sooner was I off the phone and handing it back to her he was sending texts. By the third day it was getting embarrassing. He was harassing me by proxy and in the end at my request Marcia left her phone in our room whenever we went out. All that aside, we had a blast. Vegas was all that it should be. Busy, loud, gaudy, crazy and such fun. Looking back it seemed that we never stopped laughing although it appeared I must have used up my quota of laughter because on my return home it came to an abrupt halt.

He came to pick me up at the airport, pushing people out of the way at arrivals to get to me, lifted me up, swung me round and smothered me in kisses. By the time we'd hit the M4 with Chiswick in our sights the mood was sourer than the Margaritas I'd been sipping round the pool in Vegas. He'd started off by asking me if I'd had a nice time. When I answered honestly that we'd had a blast he went completely on the turn with me. Asking me bizarre questions and making off the wall accusations. In the end my patience wore so thin that I think it finally died of starvation.

'I've just about had enough of you Mark'.

I wasn't looking at him, instead staring straight ahead focusing on a speck of bird shit on the windscreen. My voice was calm although my hands were shaking slightly.

'What the fuck is your problem? 'I asked, trying to keep my voice under control.

He gave no answer and I realised I had the advantage in this situation. He was driving. Therefore no opportunity for his usual reaction. Nothing to smash up, nowhere to run to. I had him trapped and I rather liked it.

'Come on, tell me. I want to know what gives you the right to treat me like I'm your possession?'

Still no reaction from him and by now I was on a roll. 'If you truly loved me you wouldn't act like this, you would..... ' my words were cut short as Mark swerved the car across two lanes pulling in front of a car that was doing about 70 mph in the fast lane. Mark accelerated and left the fuming driver beeping his horn and making wanker gestures.

My calm composure deserted me in an instant.

'Mark, slow down for gods sake, you'll kill us both.'

My pleading made it worse. His hands gripped the wheel tighter and his right foot went further to the floor. It was as if he was in a trance. I shut my eyes and began to scream, no words, just very loud screams. If I was going to die I didn't want to go quietly.

After what felt like 5 minutes but in reality was probably about 10 seconds I felt the car slow down. Opening my eyes I had never felt so happy to see a traffic jam.

The nutcase sitting next to me was punching the steering wheel over and over muttering away to himself through clenched teeth. It struck me how ugly he looked at that moment and I just had to get away from him. The traffic was at a standstill and we were coming up to Hammersmith Broadway so I only had to navigate through the lanes to get to the pavement. I simultaneously unclipped my seat belt and opened the door. I was expecting Mark to make a grab for me and I wasn't wrong. Fortunately I was too quick for him and took great satisfaction in slamming the car door as hard as I could before darting through the cars to safety.

I could hear Mark hollering my name. He had obviously got out of the car but there was no way I was looking back. As crazy as he was I felt sure he would not abandon my car, a Porsche Boxster that he loved bombing round town in.

On the road to the left of me was the familiar sight of the

MS logo above the entrance to the store. Clearly I was in no mood for shopping but it offered a temporary sanctuary.

I walked through the doors breathing a sigh of relief. Having spent nearly 11 hours on a plane followed by 45 minutes in a car with a madman all I wanted to do was go home, have a cup of tea, a nice hot bath and get into bed. I wandered through the food department imagining what it would be like to live normally. Filling up a trolley, going home to a loved one, not being accused of having it off with the bloke behind the meat counter. Unpacking the food, preparing a meal together, eating without being interrogated if you decided to leave a potato on the plate. Having a whole set of crockery for more than a month not having to replace plates that had been smashed against the wall in unprovoked anger.

I found a coffee shop on the main road and assessed my immediate options whilst sipping a latte and picking at a Danish pastry. I had my handbag across my shoulder which contained the usual amount of rubbish. Thankfully within the rubbish were my keys, purse and passport.

I was slipping ever so slightly into drama queen mode thinking I needed my passport. I'd only just used it to get back in the country, last thing I wanted was to use it to get out again.

I rummaged in my bag and found an old receipt and a pen which I used to compile a list of options:

- Get bus home, Mark waiting for me NO NO NO
- Get train to Patsy and Ron's, worrying them AGAIN
- Find the nearest pub and drink too much
- Check into a hotel for the night (Travelodge in Battersea a possibility???)
- Find phone box call Mark and say what??????? FUCK OFF
- Throw myself off of Battersea Bridge on the way to

Travelodge

What a very sad list it was turning out to be.
On the napkin under my pastry I began a more positive one.

- Get a taxi home
- Ask Mark to leave AGAIN
- Call police if he refuses
- Wave goodbye as they arrest him and drive him away in a police car
- Have a cup of tea in the bath
- Go to bed ALONE

It actually turned out to be a combination of the two lists.

I did get a taxi back to the flat after stopping off for a couple of glasses of wine in a nice pub on the river. I called Mark from a phone box to ask him to leave the flat before I got there. I knew he wouldn't leave but it was worth a try. By now it was about five hours since we had left Heathrow and as I climbed the stairs a feeling of utter exhaustion overwhelmed me. I felt weak, not only in body but in mind and spirit. I didn't even have the energy to find my keys. I used the lions head door knocker that we had bought in an antique shop in the Cotswolds only a few weekends before. Was it possible that we had enjoyed such a perfect couple of days then, only for it to end up like this. He opened the door and pulled me into his arms and I allowed myself to stay there for a minute listening to his apologetic bullshit. I had no fight left in me.

For that day at least.

Eight

True to form Mark behaved like the worlds best boyfriend as he always did following "an episode". The extravagant gestures just kept on coming. Bearing in mind we had only been dating for nine months I had received gifts a wife of fifty years would have been worthy of. I had the Cartier Love bracelet in both gold and platinum. The design was a bangle with screws embedded in the metal. It came with a tiny tool that unscrewed the bangle to enable the wearer to put it on. The idea was you didn't take it off which would have been perfect if I was a lady who lunched instead of a nurse who wasn't allowed to wear any jewellery apart from studs in her ears. The rigmarole of fiddling about using a screwdriver every time I wanted to wear one of them was too much so they had been stashed away in the bottom drawer of my bedside table. Following his recent freak out he raised his game to a whole new level.

I had woken up on the Sunday morning a couple of days after my near death experience on the M4 feeling desperately in need of a swim. Of course there was no argument from Mark. I could rely on him to be as nice as pie for the next few weeks until the wires in his brain got tangled up again. I swam more lengths than I intended and indulged in a long hot shower that left me pink and glowing.

Arriving back at the flat I was feeling refreshed and optimistic about the day ahead. I was starving after my exercise and headed straight for the kitchen calling out Mark's name on the way. I found him cutting a lemon into wedges. On the table there was a plate of smoked salmon, a selection of cheese, a fruit platter, pastries, pink champagne, fruit juice, a huge bunch of dusky pink roses and a small robin egg blue box that women the world over would recognise.

'Oh Mark, how lovely 'I gasped.

I had to hand it to him, he always knew how to pull it out of the bag. While I sat at the table waiting for him to join me, I offered up a prayer to my darling mother asking that the box from Tiffany contained earrings.

As Mark reached for the box and went down on bent knee I knew my prayer had gone unanswered.

'Cleo, my beautiful girl.'

A slight pause for effect.

'I know what a complete pain I am but I absolutely love and adore you and want you to be my wife.'

He removed the lid of the box to reveal a rather lovely diamond solitaire that under normal circumstances I would have been happy to wear.

Sadly circumstances were far from normal and the ring was going nowhere near my finger. I had a split second to decide how to deliver my refusal. The honest answer would have been something along the lines of 'Are you fucking kidding me? 'whilst laughing my head off. But I'm not that cruel so I decided to let him down gently reminding him that he was actually still married to another woman and he could go to prison for bigamy. I was trying to inject a little humour into the conversation but it got no laughs from him. In actual fact there appeared to be tears forming in his eyes that in turn choked me up a bit. He was still on his bent knee and I pulled his head onto my lap.

I spoke softly to him pressing my mouth onto his head, his hair tickling my lips.

'Now's not the right time for us baby. You have to sort yourself out. We love each other and that's enough for the time being.'

That proposal turned out to be the first of many over the ensuing years. Each time the answer remained the same. He cooked me dinner once and spelt out MARRY ME in french beans. To date I am the owner of three diamond rings, 1 gold ingot with 'Be my wife 'inscribed on the back and a china mug with Mrs Palmer printed across it.

He put my first refusal down to the fact he was still married to wife number two. He began divorce proceedings convincing himself that I would start planning our wedding once he had received the decree nice. I let him carry on in ignorant bliss.

Our first Christmas together came and went without incident and we saw in the new year with pink champagne and promises from Mark to behave himself.

February of 2003 was Mark's Dad's birthday. We were invited along with Mark's brother John and his wife Kerry for lunch on the Orient Express.

I liked Mark's parents. They were good company and they had always made me feel part of the family. I was looking forward to it up until a couple of days before when I felt a burning sensation whilst passing urine. I had suffered on and off with cystitis since my teenage years and I had learnt that if I treated the symptoms early enough it prevented a full blown attack. I popped out on my lunch break from work to the chemist to pick up the over the counter medication I needed. It was a foul tasting powder that balanced out the alkaline in the urine. Four sachets a day over forty eight hours usually did the trick.

Unfortunately I was so busy at work that after downing the first sachet with two fingers holding my nose to avoid tasting it I went for the rest of my shift without taking another one. By the time I got home that night I was so knackered I fell into bed with an unwashed face, unbrushed teeth and a bladder full of bacteria. Waking up the following morning I felt quite unwell. I was hardly ever ill but on the rare occasion I was, Mark was very sympathetic. He insisted I stay home from work and said he would take the day off to look after me.

'Mark, I've got three days off after today. I'll be fine once I take the medication. You get yourself off to work and I'll see you tonight.'

I made sure I drank lots of water and took the sachets at regular intervals through the day.

The other thing I had to do was avoid sex which was incredibly difficult with Mark for a partner. To say he had an insatiable appetite when it came to sex was an understatement. Fortunately we were pretty well matched in that department and sex was the one subject we never argued about. Work was so hectic that day that I hardly had a chance to feel unwell, but by the time I got home I was really struggling. Mark had prepared a meal that looked and smelt delicious but I had no appetite.

'Oh my poor baby 'he cooed. 'I hate to see you unwell.'

I pulled a sad face at him and sighed 'I think I'm going to take a couple of paracetamol and have an early night. I want to feel better for our day out tomorrow.'

As I bent down to open the drawer where we kept our medicine box he came up behind me and wrapped his arms around my waist. I could feel his erection through his jeans as he leant into me. I was still wearing my scrub top and his hands slipped up through the bottom of the loose fitting garment to find my breasts encased in a very unattractive sports bra.

'Er Mark, please don't.'

I tried to stand up but he kept me down by bearing his weight on me.

'We don't have to have penetration 'he murmured.

'Oh thanks for being so considerate 'I commented sarcastically.

I pushed myself up and this time he allowed me to stand.

'The last thing I want to do right now is give you a blow job. I don't feel well Mark, I'm off to bed.'

He followed shortly after and climbed into bed pulling me into him. I pretended to be asleep in case he started getting amorous again. I needn't have worried. He softly moved my hair out of the way, kissed my neck and whispered that he loved me before his gentle snores were the only sound I could hear. During the night there was the most amazing thunderstorm. It woke me up but Mark lay next to me undisturbed. Rolls of thunder preceded the lightning that illuminated the bedroom and framed Mark's face in an ethereal light. As I lay there propped up on my elbow staring at him, his beauty all but took my breath away. I knew at that moment how difficult it would be to live my life without this man it.

The first pee of the day after I awoke the next morning was so painful. Try to imagine twenty wasps stinging your fanny and that might give you an idea of the pain I was in. The last thing I wanted to do was socialise in a cramped space whilst eating a meal and drinking alcohol. There was no getting out of it so I dosed myself up with paracetamol and put on a brave face. We had dressed up for the occasion and as we were leaving the flat we met our neighbour on the stairs.

'Oooh, look at you two looking like a couple of film stars.'

We hailed a cab to take us to Victoria where we met up with the rest of the fam.

There were lots of ooh's and ahhh's about how lovely everyone had scrubbed up. From the moment we stepped into the carriage Mark had the devil in him. We sat opposite each other on a table for two whilst next to us Paul and Elaine shared a table for four with John and Kerry. As soon as we sat down his hand was under the table connecting with my legs, prising them apart as my knee length black dress rode up towards my hips.

He had watched me get dressed that morning and was fully aware that my legs were encased in hold ups with a border of lace resting on my thighs. When the waiter came to our table with a glass of champagne for each of us I attempted a very weak refusal. It took about two seconds for Mark to change my mind and even though I knew I was going to pay dearly later on, that first sip went down a treat. Mark continued with his fumbling under the table and I gave him a look hoping to convey the message to calm down which he did through the starter and main course.

With the alcohol ban broken by the champagne it seemed pointless to refuse the wine on offer. I could feel myself getting nicely tipsy and by the time desserts were being ordered I had all but forgotten about my poor bladder. I excused myself from the table to use the bathroom before my lemon posset accompanied by a shortbread thin arrived.

It was occupied so I stood waiting, swaying slightly a combination of the moving train and the wine. I felt a hand on my backside and turned to see Mark in front of me, eyes glistening, smile cheeky. He kissed me, the gentle touch of his tongue finding mine. His erection straining against his suit trousers. We pulled apart as we heard the bathroom door being unlocked. We smiled at the elderly lady as we let her pass by us, back to her carriage. Within seconds we were in there with the door locked. The small sink was encased in a vanity unit that was the perfect height for me to lean on. I pulled my dress up as Mark released his cock through his zip. For a fleeting second I thought about refusing him. I knew the consequences of sex and cystitis, but I could not resist him and I'm not sure he would have let me. He didn't enter me straight away, instead concentrating on kissing my neck and pinching my nipples through the woollen fabric of my dress. I sat back on the unit hoping it would hold my weight and raised my legs up around his waist. He used one hand to put his cock inside me and the other to grab my hair which up to that point had been in a neat bun. It was quick and satisfying.

We walked back to our carriage on a sex high. My legs felt weak, wobbling not from the high heels I was wearing but from the orgasm that had shuddered through every part of my body moments before. With glazed eyes, smudged lipstick and my hair free from its bun I sat back down to eat my dessert. Attempting some sort of damage limitation I took a sachet of medication just before going to bed that night.

Unfortunately to no avail. I woke in the morning with crippling back pain and knew I had to get to my doctors as soon as possible. Mark drove me even though it was only a five minute walk. I could barely put one foot in front of the other. I must have looked as bad as I felt. The receptionist made a call as soon as she saw me and ushered me straight through the waiting area to room number 7. Everything moved in fast motion after that. I was asked to produce a urine sample which brought tears to my eyes as it stung so much. As soon as Dr Gupta stuck his strip of litmus paper in my muddy coloured wee he informed me he was calling an ambulance. Three hours later I was back where I worked. Not on the right floor or in the right clothes, but in a hospital gown lying on a bed in the urology department with an intravenous antibiotic pumping through my veins.

The infection in my bladder had spread to my kidneys (hence the back pain). There was blood and high levels of protein in my urine and my temperature was high. Despite that fact I was shivering. It got so bad my teeth began to chatter which alarmed Mark who was sitting on the chair next to the bed holding my hand.

'I'm freezing 'I managed to say through chattering teeth.

'Cleo, stop it, stop shaking for fucks sake.'

He grabbed a spare blanket from the bottom of the bed and threw it over me whilst shouting out 'Nurse nurse'. I was rigid with coldness and I could see the panic in Mark's face. He moved quickly to the bed to the left of me and dragged the cover off the lady who was sleeping soundly. He did the same to the patient in the bed opposite who was very much awake.

'Oi, what the bleeding ell dya fink you're doin? 'the old girl shouted whilst waving her hands. 'If I could get out of this bed I'd effing have you, cheeky little bastard.'

He took no notice and ran back to throw the blankets over me reassuring me he would get me warmed up. It was difficult for me to talk with my teeth banging around in my mouth. I tried to speak but instead bit down on my tongue. Instantly I tasted blood. Mark screamed out' Oh my God', and ran out of the ward informing anyone that would listen that blood was pouring out of my mouth. He returned a minute later with a nurse in tow obviously looking for the patient who was haemorrhaging. Instead she found a mound of blankets and my head poking out of the top with a touch of blood on my bottom lip.

The old girl still lying uncovered on her bed started to rant about Mark being a thieving git. If I hadn't have felt so rough I would have laughed. The nurse ignored her and removing the blankets she spoke in a gentle tone explaining she was going to cover me in a light sheet instead reassuring me that the shaking would soon pass. She instructed me to relax and take some nice deep breaths.

Within a few minutes my breathing was steady and my body was still.

'Fucking hell Cleo, you frightened the life out of me 'said Mark sitting back on the chair next to the bed clutching my hand.

I didn't answer, all I wanted to do was close my eyes and drift off.

There was more chance of a gymnast having tits than getting any sleep on that ward. What with the health care assistant coming round every five minutes (at least that's what if felt like) to do observations, the old girl shouting and farting in the bed opposite and the cleaner who kept banging my bed with her V shaped sweeper I gave up. I sent Mark down to the hospital shop to get me some magazines. He came back with Take a Break and Vogue. I spent the next hour looking at pictures of models with eating disorders wearing clothes and jewellery that cost more than my yearly salary. Then it was on to Take a Break. And I thought I had problems.

Later that afternoon, the doctors carried out their rounds. Mark was still by my bedside when a rather handsome doc that I wasn't familiar with introduced himself and checked my notes. He asked if it was okay for Mark to stay in the cubicle. He had some questions that he thought I may want to answer in confidence.

'Oh, that's fine for him to stay 'I said looking more at Mark than the doctor.

It felt strange to be the one answering the questions rather than asking them. He jotted a couple of notes down as I was talking then asked me if I'd had more than one sexual partner in recent months.

'I appreciate that is a difficult question but we do have to rule out sexually transmitted diseases.'

I sensed a sudden change in Mark's demeanour. His eyes darted between me and the doctor.

'Well it's not a difficult question for me 'I replied smiling slightly, trying to make light of it.' Just the one 'I nodded towards Mark.

The doctor, picking up on my attempt to lighten the mood smiled at Mark.

'Silly question? 'he asked Mark.

The words were left hanging in the air a second too long before Mark realised he was expected to answer.

'Oh, of course, yes, yes 'he answered clearly flustered.

Instinct should have kicked in then. Maybe it did and I ignored it. Maybe it was because I was unwell and not firing on all cylinders. Maybe the idea of Mark being unfaithful to me was so utterly inconceivable that I chose not to process the fact that he was sitting next to me with beads of sweat breaking out on his forehead and his right leg jerking up and down in time to a beat that only he could hear.

Two weeks I spent on that bloody ward. Mark visited everyday, making the most of the visiting hours which started at three in the afternoon and finished at eight at night. I told him it wasn't necessary, but he insisted on staying for the whole five hours. Lying in my uncomfortable bed late at night in those few hazy minutes before my sleeping tablet kicked in I would fantasise that Mark failed to turn up for visiting hours the next day and the day after that and nobody could locate him and that he vanished without trace and I would drift off to sleep with a tiny smile hovering on my lips.

Nine

By the end of March I was feeling 100% better albeit with warnings from the urology consultant that it could take a year to recover fully, I made a decision that I was sticking to come hell or high water. I told Mark he had to move out. I felt somewhat sorry for him when I delivered the news. He looked confused and I could hardly blame him. We had actually been getting on fine. He was so happy that I was better and his mood swings were on the decrease. Maybe it was because at that stage my physical health was more important to me than my mental health. Being so ill had scared me and I blamed Mark for putting my health at risk. Of course I also had a part to play. He didn't rape me on the Orient Express, I was more than willing and I knew the consequences. But it wasn't just that one careless episode that had affected my well being. There were other contributing factors.

I slept erratically depending on what mood Norman Bates was in before we went to bed. My diet which had always been very healthy had been infiltrated by his diet of take aways, crisps, cheese and chocolate. I would inform him that we were having a stir fry for dinner that night and he would come home from work with a large tub of Häagen Dazs in my favourite flavour knowing full well I wouldn't rest until I'd scoffed the lot. Even my skin care regime had been sabotaged. He would follow me into the bathroom at night questioning 'why was I using all that shit on my face?', wasting time that could be spent in bed with him. I craved time to myself. He seemed to be at home more than he was at work. My flat which had always seemed so light and spacious felt like the walls were closing in on me. I felt suffocated by his near constant presence and declarations of love.

It was very difficult to explain my reasons for wanting him

to go without hurting his feelings. In the end we agreed to compromise. He would stay with me on Tuesday, Thursday and Saturday nights, spending the remaining nights in Putney with good ol Ma and Pa until he found a place of his own. This arrangement obviously suited me more than it did Mark. He hated the fact that at thirty nine years of age he was living with his parents. He hated that both his Mum and Dad smoked like chimneys. He hated that all he had was a tiny grotty room in the attic with an ensuite shower that was so small he had to step into it sideways. But most of all he hated the fact that I was out of his control for four nights a week.

That I was still without a mobile phone only made matters worse for him. If I went out after work on the nights I didn't see him I would come home to find the answering machine full. Every message would be from him, starting off nicely but by the sixth or seventh message all traces of niceness replaced by anger and suspicion. I took great pleasure in listening to those messages. Mark's voice would fill the room.

'Where the fuck are you Cleo?'

'Here my darling in this fabulous flat just about to run a bath 'I would sing back.

Or 'You better call me back before eleven o'clock or else'. I would laugh out loud.

'Or else what you fucking head case 'I was answering an answer machine, calling him a head case...

The happier I was with our new arrangements the more despondent he became. He was particularly miserable on Sunday's. It was torture, from the moment we woke up till the glorious moment in the evening when he left to go back to Putney.

'Why are you more of a pain on Sunday? 'I asked him after I had spent half the day cooking a rib of beef with a horseradish crust, dauphinoise potatoes and a ton of vegetables only for him to say he wasn't hungry.

'Am I? 'he answered knowing full well it was true.

'Yes, and you know you are. What's the point of being together if you're going to spoil it. I'd rather be at Patsy and Ron's having lunch with people who actually laugh and interact and show warmth and kindness instead of walking on eggshells around you.'

'Walking on eggshells eh, is that how you feel around me? ' he asked with a sneer on his face.

I could see from his reaction that this conversation was shaping up to be the prelim for what could potentially be a big fight.

'Yes, that's how I feel around you. You're always smashing eggs Mark. Don't you ever get tired of it, don't you ever wish to just be at peace with yourself and people around you?'

I did not get the reaction I was expecting. He didn't even raise his voice. He took both my hands in his and with tears brimming in his eyes he told me how he wished so desperately for peace in his mind.

'I hate Sunday's, they're a reminder that the next day is the beginning of another week living apart from you and that I won't see you till Tuesday.'

'It's only for the time being, until you sort yourself out 'I reassured him.

May God forgive me, in my head I was praying he didn't sort himself out anytime soon. I was enjoying having time to myself.

I know people must wonder why I stayed with him. Hell, I wondered why I stayed with him. I fell in and out of love with him on a regular basis. Cuckoos in a clock had nothing on me. In out, in out, in out. I could adore him in the morning and loathe him by midday.

None of the reasons why women stayed in abusive relationships applied to me. Not one.

There were no kids to consider.

I was financially independent and gainfully employed.

I owned my own property.

Despite his attempts to alienate me from my friends he had failed and I remained close to them.

My confidence had not been dented. I knew my worth. I was reasonably attractive, reasonably intelligent, reasonably young. Overall a generally reasonable human being who was not afraid to be without a partner. Without blowing my own trumpet I think I would have found it relatively easy to meet another partner if I so wanted.

I was healthy (just about).

I was well aware of his attempts to manipulate / bully / coerce me, and I gave in only if it suited me.

And the most important one of all was that I was completely unafraid of him.

I stayed in the relationship because when it was good it was fantastically amazingly wonderful and I loved the bones of him. Not forgetting the mind blowing sex that I was loathe to live without.

We settled into a routine that worked for me and for the most part Mark as well. It wasn't set in stone that he would only stay on designated nights and at times it felt like he lived with me permanently. As long as he was acting like a normal human being I was happy but as soon as he stepped out of line I had our agreed arrangement to fall back on.

Physically I was back in shape but I felt in need of a mental detox. Mark thought talk like that was, and I quote 'a load of old bollocks'. I wasn't looking for approval or permission and set about finding a retreat where I could give my brain a rest. I imagined doing yoga at sunset on a mountain overlooking an ocean, meditating with the smell of joss sticks in the air. Eating wholesome foods with my fingers whilst sitting cross legged on a giant cushion in an open space decorated with lanterns. I contacted an old friend of my mum's who never grew out of her hippie stage. She would know where to recommend. She'd spent the last thirty years roaming from one country to another in search of peace and enlightenment. Aurora (Beverly to her parents) was delighted to hear from me and we arranged to meet in a Vietnamese cafe that had just opened in Kensington.

Sitting in the window of the cafe, her long dark hair hi-lighted with streaks of grey, spread out over her shoulders, down her back touching the chair. Large dangly earrings, skin on her forearms barely visible through the mass of bangles and colourful bits of cotton tied round her wrists. Rings on every finger and both thumbs. Her ample bosom was displayed in all its glory in a wrap around paisley dress in various shades of green. She jangled as she got up and came towards me. She smelt of Opium by YSL and her lips were the colour of Damson plums.

'My sweet girl, how lovely to see you 'she exclaimed kissing me on both cheeks and hugging me tightly.

Releasing me, she held my face between her hands and I felt the cool metal from her fingers on my cheeks.' I see pain in your eyes, a sadness that you don't deserve'.

'Oh, Aurora, you never change do you 'I said laughing as we sat down.

'It's a gift darling, to recognize pain and help people heal.'

She looked at me with scepticism as I explained that the opposite was true. That I was happy and in a good place and just needed some space to clear my head.

Over lotus tea and slices of dragon fruit sprinkled with caraway seeds she gave me the lowdown on various retreats from Ireland to India and discussed all things spiritual.

We parted in the street with warm hugs and a reminder from Aurora that my chakras were out of alignment in particular my solar plexus and third eye.

That evening I told Mark of my plans to spend a week away in May on a small Greek island. He took the news well, especially when I told him it was a female only resort.

Before we knew it, Mark was driving me to Gatwick to

catch an early morning flight. We had been getting on so well that I found myself regretting booking the trip. I was going to miss him. We kissed and hugged at the entrance to departures and it crossed my mind how desperate I had been to get away from him last October. Guilt pricked at my conscience and I promised I would try to call him as soon as I got there from the landline.

'I love you so much 'were his parting words as he stood blowing kisses in the air as I walked towards security.

After a four hour flight and a one hour boat trip I finally arrived at Healing the Heart spiritual retreat.

When Aurora suggested it, I was slightly dubious. I imagined a group of lost souls, damaged beyond repair, desperate for help. She assured me it was nothing like that.

'Darling, it will do you the power of good to be in the company of like minded people.'

'But my heart doesn't need healing and I'm not sure I want to spend a week with a bunch people whose hearts do 'I answered, a whinging edge to my voice.

'Go, she said with a twinkle in her eye, 'You will thank me I promise'.

And thank her I did. There wasn't a miserable person amongst us and in between omming, deep breathing, extreme contortion of my body and emptying my mind we actually had quite good fun.

The only fly in the ointment concerned Mark (as usual). I had asked to use the landline on my first day to let him know I had arrived safely. My request was granted but I was informed that communication with the outside world was discouraged and guests who were in possession of mobiles were kindly asked to leave them in a safe at reception. When he answered my heart missed a beat.

'Hi baby, how are you? 'he asked.

'Missing you madly 'I replied with genuine feeling.

We had a warm and loving conversation that ended with

both of us near to tears at the thought of saying goodbye. I promised I would find a way to call him in the next couple of days. As luck would have it Susie my allocated room mate was not comfortable handing in her mobile and she was happy for me to use it on one condition. In return I had to accompany her on illicit fag breaks which we took in a small cove at the end of a fifteen minute treacherous walk down the side of a steep hill. While Susie sucked greedily on her forbidden Silk Cut I punched in Mark's number which I knew off by heart. After a short delay an automated voice informed me the phone was switched off and to try again later. It struck me as odd that he would have his phone off knowing I could be calling at any time.

I tried twice more, once in the afternoon and again in the evening. Was I worried? Not worried exactly but I wanted to speak to him. I missed him.

When I rang the following day and got the same message I was beginning to feel ever so slightly pissed off. Not wanting to waste the money and effort I had put in to cleansing my soul of bad thoughts I decided to resign myself to the fact that I would not attempt to contact him from Greece again. There was only a couple of days to go before I would be reunited with him anyway.

And what a reunion it was. We spent two days in bed with hardly any sleep, Billy Joel playing in the background as we made love in between eating take away pizzas and drinking wine.

Ten

It was a big birthday for Mark that year. August was the month he would turn forty. My birthday was the day after his. I would be thirty five. He insisted he didn't want a fuss and would rather be away for the celebration. That suited me. We decided on a four night break so my annual leave could go towards a longer holiday later on in the year. Unable to decide on a destination I went into the bedroom and returned with a rolled up map of the world and a small metal tin. The map was disintegrating at the edges and particles of dust filled the air as I unrolled it and laid it on the floor. Mark put his hands on two corners and I held down the opposite side.

My mum had stuck the map on my bedroom wall in our council flat in Chelsea when I was seven. She had told me about all the wonderful places we would visit when she got a better job and had a bit more money. She put a packet of drawing pins on my bedside table and sat down on my bed.

'You have to stick a pin in the map so you know where you've been, so you don't go to the same place again'.

'But Mum, what about if you want to go back to the same place? 'I asked.

She shook her head laughing at me.' Why on earth would you Cleo? There's over two hundred countries in the world and thousands of cities.'

I opened the lid of the box and took out a brass coloured pin.

Handing it to Mark I told him I was going to blindfold him and spin the map round a few times. Wherever the map was pierced was our destination. Only rule was it couldn't be somewhere we had ever been before. I pulled the blindfold down and in it went. We were off to Austria. For his birthday I bought him a rather expensive Omega watch that he'd had his eye on for a while. Even though I was financially secure Mark insisted on paying for most things. He gave me money every week towards our living expenses which were minimal as I had no mortgage. So I figured he deserved the watch. Seeing the look on his face when he opened it on the morning of his birthday in our swanky suite in a hotel in Vienna it was worth it. He showed his appreciation the best way he could.

We spent a glorious day wandering the streets of Vienna, stopping for coffee and exquisite cake and champagne and more exquisite cake. I cried with laughter at Mark seemingly petrified on one of the worlds oldest Ferris wheels, the Wiener Riesenrad. I thought he was joking when he had told me he was scared of heights. We had to go straight for a beer after that to calm him down. The next day was my turn to be spoilt. As usual he had gone all out and presented me with the now familiar red box of Cartier. Nestled in the black velvet were a pair of diamond studs that were so beautiful they took my breath away. I jumped on him and smothered him in kisses wrapping my arms and legs around him.

'Thank you, thank you, thank you 'I repeated over and over.

I could not stop smiling all day and every chance I got to glance at my reflection my eyes zoned in on those beauties resting in my lobes. Did I give a thought to the cost of them? I would be lying if I said it didn't cross my mind. I knew they must be in the region of a couple of grand. I was confused by Mark's incomings and outgoings. He didn't seem to work enough hours to earn the money he appeared to be spending. I never once heard him complain about lack of it and he certainly took great pleasure in splashing it about. I didn't want it to spoil our time away but made a note to myself that I needed to speak to him about it.

A few days after our return at the beginning of September Mark was at the flat relaxing on the sofa. I was in the kitchen preparing a salad when he called my name asking me to bring him some tissues as he was having a nose bleed. It wasn't serious and it soon stopped with a bit of pinching halfway down his nose. He was already on medication for high blood pressure following a mild heart attack when he was thirty six. I told him if it happened again he should make an appointment with the doctor. A couple of weeks later we were just about to go out shopping when his nose started bleeding but much heavier this time. Wads of kitchen roll and a firm pinch sorted it out. I asked if he had any other symptoms but he said he felt fine. To be honest he didn't look fine to me. His olive skin usually a light brown through the summer months had lost its glow leaving a sallow tinge in its place. It may have been why the dark rings under his eyes were so noticeable. He had been quiet and slightly withdrawn in the past couple of weeks. I asked if there was anything worrying him, work, Harry, his parents, money.

'Cleo, you'd never leave me would you? 'was his reply.

'What the fuck are you on about, you're worrying me now ' was my somewhat aggressive reply.

'Just answer me 'he pleaded.

Well I was hardly going to say 'yes I fantasise about it often and I probably will leave you at some point'.

'No you silly bugger, not today anyway 'I said with a wry smile.

I told him to head towards the bedroom and have a lie down while I went and got the shopping. I really needed five minutes and a strong coffee to mull over what was going on. One hour, one espresso, one latte and a lemon and white chocolate muffin later I was none the wiser. Nothing had changed between us recently. Although a little subdued he was still his usual possessive self although surprisingly there hadn't been any violent outbursts. No crockery smashed, no holes punched in doors, no accusations of giving the postman a blow job. Was he suffering with withdrawal from violence. Was he going cold turkey. Was I wasting my life trying to get to the bottom of a crazy man's mind. The only thing I was sure of at that moment was my cupboards and fridge were bare and I needed to hit the supermarket.

The following weeks saw little change in his demeanour. As I expected, he failed to make an appointment with his GP. If he had, it may have saved me from answering the phone on the evening of November fifth to hear his mother informing me that Mark had suffered a massive heart attack.

I had been on the late shift and didn't get home till about 10.00 on that Wednesday evening. I could hear the phone ringing as I turned the key in the front door but didn't rush, fully expecting the usual 'where the hell have you been? ' message from my paranoid boyfriend.

I picked it up on the last ring to hear Elaine, Mark's mum.

'Cleo, hello love, Mark's had a heart attack. He's in intensive care.'

Honestly, just like that, as if she was informing me he had tripped over and sprained his ankle. There was no point in me going to the hospital at that time of night. I knew the last thing the nurses in the ICU needed was loved ones standing around a sick patient getting in the way, asking endless questions that they couldn't answer. All they wanted to do was get on with their job without interruption.

Knowing I wouldn't be able to sleep I lay on top of the duvet without even changing out of my uniform. I imagined the phone ringing at two o'clock in the morning, answering it to hear that he had died. How would I feel? Would I collapse in a heap on the floor and scream his name over and over. Would I be lost for words, overcome by grief unable to formulate a sentence. Would I thank god it was over and appreciate the feeling of peace that washed over me. I would never know. No phone call came at two in the morning. I waited until four thirty to get up, clean my teeth and splash my face with cold water. By four forty five still in my uniform I was starting out on the three mile walk to the hospital in

Hammersmith. My natural walk had always been fast and I could have been there in thirty minutes. I forced myself to slow down, stopping to chat to the man setting up the flower stall on the corner of my road, taking long routes rather than short cuts, stopping for coffee in an all night cafe on the Fulham Road.

I arrived at the hospital just as the darkness was fading giving way to the dawn.

I took the stairs to the ICU and after giving Mark's name was buzzed through.

Before I saw him the nurse explained that he was stable and had had a good night. They were waiting to transfer him to another hospital to have a stent fitted and if everything went according to plan he would be transferred back to recover on the cardiology ward.

As soon as he saw me a huge smile lit up his pale drawn face.

'Hi babes.'

I knew in that moment if he had died I would have been devastated.

And so began the surprisingly speedy road back to recovery. In his favour was his age, his strength, his status as a non smoker and his complete denial that anything serious had actually happened to him. He was in hospital for two weeks following the fitting of the stent. Scans showed that he would have to be monitored as other valves were showing signs of deterioration. I visited everyday either before or after work depending on my shift. He had a side room on his own and I would bring him homemade food making every effort to keep it healthy. I liked going at night best when his other visitors had left and it was just the two of us. We would lay spooning on the bed watching the TV as Mark got a hard on and tried to slip his hands inside my bra.

'Stop it Mark, think of all that blood rushing around down there 'I gasped looking down at the bulge straining against the thin cotton of his shorts. If he ignored me I would threaten to tell the matron who could have given Nurse Ratched a run for her money.

For six weeks every Monday we attended cardiac rehab, a programme aimed at helping people understand their condition, make lifestyle changes to improve heart health and reduce risk of further heart problems. If I didn't know the saying 'laughter is the best medicine 'had been around for a hundred years I swear it could have originated from that group.

Bearing in mind Mark was only forty whereas the rest of the participants were in their seventies or older. There was Doris who thought she was banned from eating cheese for the rest of her life.

'What am I going to do with the two pound lump of cheddar in my fridge? It's got a sell by date of 29th of December and I wouldn't like it to go to waste.'

Barbara, seventy six, would turn up for classes in outfits that reminded me of Olivia Newton-John in Xanadu, minus the roller skates. She told us about her dancing days and how she could still do the splits and even though no-one disbelieved her she insisted on giving us a demonstration. That ended up in a groin strain for Barbara and a pulled back muscle for Kirsty the tutor, after she had to lift the red faced ex-dancer off the floor and plonk her on a chair. Arthur who was eighty on his next birthday was concerned he wouldn't be able to perform for his wife who according to him was 'very demanding in the bedroom department'.

Mark hadn't taken any of the advice seriously, least of all the recommendations regarding sex. Abstain for at least four weeks was the clear message. For me the thought of going without sex for a month was disappointing, for Mark it was devastating. When we first met he told me the longest time he had gone without it since his early twenties was three weeks. Through both his marriages he had indulged in several affairs as well as one night stands and resorted to prostitutes when he couldn't be bothered to chat a woman up.

We broke the ban on day seventeen. Before we done the dirty deed I laid down some ground rules.

1. No marathon session. Keep it to a sprint
2. One position only. Me on top. (As fit as I was I wasn't confident I could lift twenty one stone of dead weight off me if he collapsed mid thrust)
3. This was a one off until the four weeks were up
4. Glyceryl Trinitrate (GTN spray) must be on bedside table within easy reach of both parties. This medication was prescribed following his heart attack and could potentially save his life if he suffered another attack.
5. If at anytime either parties felt uncomfortable (this directed more at Mark than me) stop immediately.

I actually wrote all this down and handed it to him. He obviously didn't take any of it in, or chose to ignore it as he went on to break every rule on the list. I was glad he did. Within seconds of our bare bodies touching the only thoughts in my head were what was coming next.

Mark appeared to be making a good recovery although a discussion that we had at the rehab group was never far from my mind. Kirsty, the tutor had explained how common it was to suffer from depression following a serious illness and how important it was to address it, not to sweep it under the carpet.

And sure enough a couple of months in, after the initial joy of surviving had passed, Mark's mood swings seemed to escalate. This time I knew at least one of the reasons why. He had wrongly assumed that because he'd suffered a heart attack I would be at my flat door waiting with open arms welcoming him home. My reluctance to have him move in full time wound him up no end.

It was all quiet on the violent front though which made the moodiness somewhat easier to handle.

Eleven

In the February of 2004 we went on holiday to the Bahamas, stupidly choosing an all inclusive five star resort famed for its top quality food and high end cocktails. The last place Mark needed to be considering he was under strict orders from the hospital to lose at least four stone. It was pitiful watching him ladle low fat cauliflower soup into a bowl for a starter when he'd had to walk past plates of langoustine and crab, salami, parma ham, avocado, stuffed mushrooms and salads laced with walnuts and cheese. He sat down opposite me eyeing up my plate of goodies, salivating, then looking down at the unappetising offering in front of him. By the evening of the third day all thoughts of blocked arteries and high cholesterol had faded along with the sun on the horizon.

With promises to embark on a strict diet and exercise regime on our return he set about eating and drinking his weight in rich food and alcohol.

By then we had been on several trips together and I could count on one hand the times we got involved in conversations with other couples. It wasn't our scene. At breakfast we would ask to sit in the quietest part of the dining room as far away as possible from other guests. If we wanted to leave the hotel and they provided a courtesy bus we would swerve it and call a cab instead. The most communication would be a polite good morning, or a nod of agreement if a fellow holidaymaker commented on how hot or cold the weather was. So I was surprised when Mark left me on the sun bed one day and returned from the beach bar with my midday mudslide telling me he had got chatting to a really nice guy at the bar.

'I said we'd meet up with him and his wife for a drink this evening.'

'My god 'I said nearly choking on my drink 'he must be

nice.'

And for once Mark had shown good judgement. Gordon and his wife Rene, a retired couple in their late sixties from Surrey were brilliant company, loved a drink, swore like troopers, and liked dancing to reggae music until the early hours of the morning. Despite the age gap our personalities seemed to click and we spent most evenings with them. We had an absolute blast, so much so that at the end of their holiday we swapped numbers.

Kissing and hugging them goodbye as they pulled away from the resort in the cab taking them to the airport, I could never have guessed at the significant part they would play in our lives.

Call it holiday blues for want of a better explanation but I began to feel very unsettled on our return from the Caribbean. My job was becoming increasingly stressful. Same old NHS woes. Too many patients, not enough staff, overworked and underpaid. I thought about doing something completely different, maybe even going back to university. I made a list of things that interested me and that could possibly be incorporated in a job. Top of the list was interior design. It was Mark who suggested buying a property, doing it up and selling it on. We spent the next Saturday sitting round the table in the flat surrounded by notepads, pens and a calculator working out the best way to go about it. I can be quite impulsive and no more so than on that Saturday. I suggested to Mark that I put the flat on the market and with the proceeds buy two properties. One to live in and one to renovate.

'How about moving out a bit? 'I asked Mark.

'I could get so much more for my money in the suburbs.'

The more we discussed it the better it sounded. By ten o'clock the next morning we were driving down the A3 towards Surrey. We drove aimlessly turning in and out of streets that took our fancy hoping to see some for sale signs. By mid afternoon I had noted the name and number of several estate agents in the area who had houses on their books. We stopped off for Sunday lunch in a pub in Epsom overlooking the downs.

I could just see myself and Mark with our Barbour jackets and Hunter wellies on striding across the lush green grass, a couple of labradors at our heels.

'I'm sure that Gordon and Rene live around here somewhere 'Mark commented.

'I remember him saying they always go away when the Derby is on as it's so busy round here.'

'Give them a ring 'I said, thinking how lovely it would be to see them both.

He called and as luck would have it they were at home which Gordon explained was a five minute drive from the pub. They insisted we go round for a cup of tea after we'd finished our lunch. We were instructed not to have dessert as Rene had a couple of cakes in the fridge that needed eating.

I'm not sure what I was expecting their house to be like. I knew they were comfortably off. On holiday Rene was decked from head to toe in designer gear, from her Chanel sunglasses to her Gucci flip flops and Gordon looked like a living advert for Ralph Lauren. As soon as we turned into their private road I knew exactly what their house would be like. With his and hers cars parked on the circular drive (black Range Rover for him, white Mercedes convertible for her I guessed) I felt like we were walking onto the set of footballers wives. We were greeted with hugs and kisses and taken through to the lounge. There was more animal print in there than in the Kruger safari park. It was on every soft furnishing, every hard furnishing, on the walls and on the carpet.

'So what brings you lovely people over to this neck of the woods? 'asked Gordon as Rene fussed over us, pouring tea and cutting cake. We explained our plans and instantly gained Gordons approval.

'Optimum time to be buying out this way. Prices in London are going through the roof so great if you're selling. Bring your dough out here, you'll get shitloads for it.'

They advised us on areas to avoid, roads that were particularly nice, streets that were in the catchment area for the best schools.

'That won't apply to us. I don't want kids and as Mark has two already I'm sure he agrees 'I said laughing as I spoke.

Rene looked confused.

'I thought you told me on holiday that you only had one child 'she said directing the comment at Mark.

As Mark gave no answer, Rene continued, eager to make her point.

'Now I know I like a tipple and I can be a bit forgetful at times but I distinctly remember you telling me you only had one son. We even had a conversation about only children, you must remember it.'

Good old Rene, she wouldn't let it go, like a dog with a big old bone and I was loving every second of it, bitch that I was. Her words hung in the air as we waited for him to answer.

'Cleo's right. I do have two children. I had another child but it didn't work out with the boys mother and she refused to let me have contact with my son. He was just a toddler the last time I saw him.'

What a crock of shit. He had delivered this little speech with a pitiful expression on his face and a voice that was cracking in all the right places. It was all I could do to stop myself from giving him a round of applause for his Oscar winning performance. I was watching an actor playing a part, his audience believing every word he uttered. Apart from me obviously.

'Oh what a bloody shame 'Rene sighed. 'For the life of me, I can't understand these women who deny fathers the right to see their kids. Boys in particular as far as I'm concerned.'

Mark nodded in agreement as he put his arm round my shoulder and pulled me into his chest.

'Anyway, I couldn't think of anything worse than having another baby. It would take up too much of Cleo's time and attention that I would rather she spent on me.'

Rene and Gordon looked on with bemused approval. How should I play this I thought to myself. Go along with it, or out him and the despicable lie he always told regarding his second child. Every time we met new people he declared one son forgetting the boy in Sweden. I was not comfortable with this and told him several times to tell the truth. 'It's just easier not to mention it babes. I can't be bothered with the questions.'

Now he was adding to the lie, blaming the boy's mother for the lack of contact.

I had to sit on my hands for the rest of the conversation as the urge to slap his lying face was increasing with each word. As soon as we were in the car however the urge was back again and it was all I could do to keep the smile on my face as we pulled off the drive of our friends house waving and blowing kisses to them. As the car turned onto the road my false smile evaporated and I spoke through gritted teeth.

'If you chose to lie about your son in Sweden that's up to you but do not expect me to sit by and listen to your bullshit anymore.'

I was talking to the side of his face. He didn't take his eyes off the road, just kept staring straight ahead. Spit from my mouth landed on his cheek just above his beard line.

'Why don't you say you've got two kids? How can you lie about something like that?'

I could have asked ten more questions but the truth was I wouldn't get an answer to one of them. He had switched off. I could hear a very faint humming noise emanating from the back of his throat that would have formed a tune had I listened long enough. Humming was his wordless warning to me to shut up. Never one to heed a warning however serious the danger I ploughed on calling him every name under the sun.

I concluded with the words' The next time kids are mentioned in company I'm telling people you've got two sons.'

From that point on everything moved at a bewildering speed. The flat went on the market and within three weeks I had an offer of the asking price.

Mark's contacts in the building game and his willingness to offer backhanders to estate agents secured two perfect properties. One was a two bedroom Victorian terraced cottage with a surprisingly big garden in a cul de sac, a ten minute drive from Gordon and Rene. This property was to be my home. The second property was the 'do'er upper'. It was a two bedroom flat conversion in a rambling old Victorian house overlooking Clapham Common. It was begging for a total refurbishment and I was excited at the prospect of a new challenge. People say that moving is one of the most stressful things you will do in your lifetime, up there with death of a loved one and divorce. Not for me. It was very nearly a piece of piss.

There were no chains attached to any of the properties. The couple who lived in the cottage were emigrating to Australia. The Clapham flat had been empty for nine months. The buyer for my flat was a middle aged city banker whose family home was in Hertfordshire. He tried to convince me on his first viewing that he was looking for a 'pied-a-terre 'for during the week. On his second viewing accompanied by a rather striking Russian girl who appeared to be about half his age I realised he was buying his mistress her very own place. Lucky girl I thought, or she was until her looks faded and he found a replacement. I handed in my notice at work with mixed emotions. Excitement, trepidation, loss, gain and a general feeling of 'what the hell am I doing?'

I decided to concentrate all my energy on the refurb project as the cottage although not to my taste was ready to move into being clean and functional.

Of course it made sense for Mark to do the work but there were a couple of specialist jobs that I had to get outside contractors in to do. I had seen a technique used on walls that I wanted in the flat. The finished result actually looked like freshly plastered polished walls with subtle hints of randomly placed glitter specks. I wanted a free standing bath and we found a stunning copper bath on one of our many trips to salvage yards. It cost a fortune to have it cleaned up and prepared for modern day fittings but it was worth it. We threw all our time and energy into the flat, often staying overnight snuggled up together on a blow up bed so we could get an early start in the morning.

Much to Mark's annoyance I was still refusing to have a mobile phone, though in a slight nod to technology I bought a digital camera. I was constantly taking before and after shots, saving swatches of fabric and samples of wallpaper to create a scrapbook of our first property refurbishment together. All in all it took just under four months to complete. We had knocked our pipes out but I had enjoyed every moment of it. The completed look was stunning and I even thought about moving in myself. The original plan had been to sell it but one of Mark's contacts in a local estate agents asked if I would consider renting. When he told me how much I could get a month for it, I nearly bit his hand off. I was proud of what we had achieved and as a thank you to Mark I booked us a trip to Iceland in November.

We participated in all the usual tourist attractions, chasing the Northern Lights (obviously not fast enough as we failed to spot them), a dip in the blue lagoon that done my hair no favours whatsoever, and a whale watching trip. We saw stunning waterfalls and tiny villages with populations less than a tower block in an inner city. The beaches were not like any I had seen before and I found them quite eerie. It was as if an artist had taken a palette of three colours and painted stripes on a canvas. Black sand, grey sea, white sky. Usually I loved the outdoors, particularly anywhere costal but I felt a strong sense of foreboding standing hand in hand with Mark looking out to sea, feeling the spray of the freezing water on my face as the waves crashed down on the coarse dark sand.

'Come on 'I said 'lets get back on the coach, I'm feeling chilly.'

We took our seats and looked at our fellow tourists asking the tour guide questions and reaching down to feel the sand beneath them. They posed for pictures which reminded me we hadn't taken any at that location.

'Mark, if I go and stand over there 'I said, pointing to a small ledge jutting out of the cliff, 'can you take a couple of shots? Make sure you get the sea in.'

We got off the coach and I walked over to the ledge, waited for Mark's thumbs up and pulled a couple of silly poses followed by a sensible one. Mark was laughing as I saw him step back on the coach and take his seat. A lady from our group caught my eye and she commented that it was nothing like Brighton Beach. We chatted for a few moments before I joined Mark. As soon as I saw him I knew there was a problem. He watched me walk up the aisle towards him with what I could only describe as evil in his eyes.

'What the hell's wrong 'I questioned him, my face frowning intently.

He lifted his arm up to show me my camera dangling from his wrist. It swung backwards and forwards in front of my face.

'Yeah, what about it? 'I asked.

He slipped it off his wrist and threw it to the side of him.

'Oi 'I raised my voice slightly. 'Be careful you idiot.'

I picked it up and asked what the problem was. He snatched it from my hand and started pressing buttons. Here we go again I thought to myself. I had no idea what he was going on about but I was pretty sure it was going to be absurd. Then he was holding the screen in front of my face jabbing at an image which I couldn't make out due to his finger covering most of it.

'Calm down, you fucking lunatic and give it to me 'I said grabbing it from him.

And there it was, the reason Mark saw fit to look at me as if I had just massacred his entire family. A picture of me and Dave in the bathroom of the Clapham flat. Dave was the guy who installed the copper bath. He took pictures for his portfolio and I took one for my scrapbook. I had set the timer on the camera and placed it on the shelf. We stood either side of the bath holding our arms out in a gesture of presentation looking very happy with ourselves which we were entitled to be. We weren't even touching each other. I looked at Mark and laughed, shook my head in disbelief and asked him if he was actually being serious. The grip on my forearm and the way he yanked me down to sit next to him told me he was.

'I fucking knew there was something going on between you two 'he hissed through clenched teeth.

'No wonder you arranged for him to install that bath when I wasn't there. How long has it been going on? Did you sleep with him in the flat?'

'Mark' I pleaded, 'please stop, you know what you're saying is not true. How can you even think that?'

But it was too late, he had switched off from me. I couldn't reach him in that mood. He continued with his paranoid accusations for the entire ninety minute journey back to the hotel. They were so ludicrous that I had to admire his imagination. There I was, under the impression that he was an ill educated builder yet his ramblings were proof that had he taken exams he could have gained at least a B plus in

English Literature O Level.

I didn't feel intimidated or threatened on the coach. He was hardly going to attack me in front of a group of tourists in a foreign country. In fact I was just pissed off that a trip that up until that point had been fantastic was, through no fault of my own about to go tits up.

Twelve

We arrived back at the hotel and went straight to our room. I had no intention of spending one more second than was necessary with the lunatic. I intended to have a quick shower, change my clothes and head out on my own. Best laid plans and all that. As soon as we were in the room Mark stripped off all his clothes and got into bed. He curled up on his side which was not his usual sleeping position at all. He reminded me of a wounded bear which made me want to lay next to him and take care of him but I was so angry and more to the point he didn't deserve it. I went into the bathroom and locked the door which under normal circumstances I would have left open. Seconds later he was thumping on the door demanding to know why I'd locked myself in and what the fuck was I doing. With the comforting security of a thick slab of wood between us I thought I could risk a slightly cocky answer.

'Er let me think, what would I possibly be doing in a bathroom? I'm not sure whether to play Beethovens Moonlight Sonata, shoot a few hoops, knit a scarf, bake some muffins or sit on the toilet and have a massive fucking dump.'

I'm not sure what reaction I was expecting but it wasn't for Mark's fist to come through the door that's for sure. Obviously it wasn't a slab of wood dividing us but two sheets of MDF.

I screamed and he roared whilst reaching down to turn the lock. As the door opened I ducked underneath his out stretched arms and made for the room door but he was too quick for me. My heart was beating out of my chest and my legs were shaking. I was swinging my arms about blindly hoping to inflict some sort of pain on him. He was telling me to calm down, assuring me he wasn't going to hurt me. Over and over he kept repeating calm down until I made my way to the bed and sunk down into the mattress. There was a moment of composure from us both before I took a deep breath and told him that I didn't think it was possible for us to carry on anymore.

'We just can't keep doing this, it has to stop 'I said.

If Mark had been looking for a trigger to explode those words were surely it. He reached for the first object he could find which happened to be a rather large television on top of a chest of drawers. He smashed it into the long mirror hanging on the wall. Shards of glass went everywhere. Next he dropped the TV on the floor and used the chair from the desk to smash the screen. Over and over he brought the chair down until there was nothing left of it apart from the base. He pulled the bedside lamps out of the sockets and made his way to the bathroom where he dropped them in the bath. I will never forget the sounds he was making, half human, half animal, though I'm not sure what animal. I was still sitting on the bed praying to whoever was listening to let this be over. I thought it was safer for me not to say anything or do anything. Above his wailing I heard a steady banging from the bathroom. From my position on the bed I couldn't see in there so I risked moving, feet crunching over the shattered mirror. Thank god I'd left my boots on.

Never had I seen such a sorry sight. The man I loved and adored standing feet apart, bent over, bare arsed with his balls swinging between his legs smashing his head rhythmically against the edge of the sink. I cried out in shock and went to him begging him to stop. I put my hands on his shoulders and used all my strength to prevent him smashing his head down again. Just as it seemed I had some control over the situation, there was more thumping only this time it was coming from outside on the door to our room.

'Is everything okay in there? 'a stern voice with an Icelandic accent shouted into the room.

I was surprised it had taken someone that long to get

there.

Under no circumstances did I want anyone to enter the room at that moment. There was no way we could cover the damage up but I felt it may soften the blow somewhat if I at least tided up what I could.

'We're fine thank you 'I said in my best I've got it all under control voice.

'There have been complaints about the noise, so please keep it down.'

'I do apologise. There won't be anymore noise tonight I can assure you.'

I breathed a sigh of relief when I heard footsteps retreating back down the corridor.

I felt like I was back in AE that night. Laying cold flannels on Marks head in a feeble attempt to prevent any brusing, picking out shards of glass from the soles of his feet with my eyebrow tweezers. Rubbing his back as he vomited into the toilet after he looked at the room and saw the destruction he had caused. Somehow we made it through the night. I cleared the bath of the smashed lamps and cleaned any spots of blood I came across with shower gel. I washed the tiles down with one of my socks and made sure the toilet was vomit free. I used the clothes brush in the wardrobe to sweep the glass up and by ten o'clock that night the bathroom was back to normal. Mark was on a come down from his manic high and after having a shower lay on the bed watching me attempting to restore the room back to its former glory. He had wanted to help of course, considering it was his mess but I insisted he rest. All he kept saying was how sorry he was and breaking down in tears. By now my sympathy cup was empty so I just kept telling him to get some sleep. In the end I had to admit defeat. I couldn't repair a broken mirror or a smashed TV and chair. I piled the rubbish as best I could in the corner of the room and decided to wait till the morning when we checked out to inform the staff. I shuddered to think how much the damage was going to cost. Iceland was expensive. We found that out when Mark bought one small beer, one bottle of water and a toasted cheese sandwich and had to hand over the equivalent of twenty two pounds for the pleasure.

On checking out I explained how the room had been left and we were willing to pay whatever it cost to replace items. The manager was called, he assessed the damage and concluded that the equivalent of a thousand pounds should cover the costs. We were in absolutely no position to argue or negotiate. I was relieved we were leaving without handcuffs on our wrists. No drama, no police, no aggro. No more trips away with psychologically damaged individuals who smash up hotel rooms in a bid to vent their anger.

On the flight home I really felt a sense that it was the end for Mark and I. Surely he could not ignore the fact that the trigger for his horrendous behaviour was the fact that I had said we couldn't carry on together. If he thought that behaving like a madman would change my feelings he was very much mistaken. If anything it drove me on to stick to my word. Normally if we went away anywhere he would always come back and stay with me for a couple of nights. I would get his washing done and he would settle back into the routine of dividing his time between Putney and my place. When we arrived back at Gatwick I made it clear we would be ordering two cabs.

'Really? 'was his response.

'Yes, really 'was my reply.

If I'm honest I did feel sorry for him having to go back to his parents. He was a grown man in his forties still living in his childhood home. But, it was his own fault. He could not expect me to welcome him into my home with such unpredictable behaviour. My cab arrived first.

'Cleo, you will never know how sorry I am or how much I love you 'he said as he enveloped me as the driver put my case in the boot.

'Oh, but I do Mark. You're so so sorry and you love me so so much but somehow it's just not quite enough to stop the craziness is it?'

I felt utterly drained and could not wait to get home. I didn't even look back as the driver manoeuvred through the lanes that would lead me to freedom.

What a short-lived freedom that turned out to be. By eight o'clock that night he was hammering on my door, unable to use his keys as I had left mine in the lock. In a very loud voice he declared his undying love through the letterbox. True to form I answered the door telling myself it was because I didn't want the neighbours disturbed but the truth was I missed him and loved him and wanted him and I was caught up in a cycle of love, lust and lunacy.

We spent Christmas of that year with our darling friends Rene and Gordon. Talk about do it in style. There were twenty guests made up of their family and friends. Rene employed a small army of staff to ensure every aspect of the festive season had been covered. From a snow machine in the garden to catering staff offering champagne and canapés on arrival to silver service waitresses serving a five course dinner to fireworks and a real live Father Christmas delivering presents from Molton Brown, Mulberry and Tiffany. A DJ was set up in a marquee in the garden and we danced into Boxing Day. We stayed overnight and in the morning I awoke early gagging for a glass of water and some caffine. I made my way down to the kitchen which looked as if nothing had ever been cooked in it. The staff had worked into the early hours of the morning to get it looking spick and span. Rene was already there spooning coffee beans into a percolator. She greeted me with a croaky 'Good morning love'. With eyes bleary and hands shaking slightly, she asked if I wanted a black coffee or a hair of the dog. The latter was mildly tempting but I felt my overworked liver could do with a rest. We sunk ourselves into the huge sofa overlooking the frost encrusted lawn, a weak sun straining through the patchy clouds.

'So, did you enjoy yourself then? 'Rene asked.

'One of the best Christmas Days I've ever had 'I answered honestly. 'I've just realised why my calves are aching so much. I haven't danced like that for a while.'

'God 'Rene exclaimed, 'talking of that, did you see the way Mark was looking at you when you were dancing. I thought he was going to crush the stem of the champagne glass he was holding when Donnie joined you in the twist.'

A vision came to mind of myself and Donnie, Gordon's older brother, a seventy eight year old man who reminded me of everyone's favourite grandad, holding hands and twisting as low as we dared to Chubby Checker.

'You do realise 'she continued, 'that Mark never takes his eyes off of you?'

It was a statement rather than a question. I shrugged my shoulders.

'I mean, never ever 'she reiterated.

'I suppose I'm used to it now so I don't take any notice 'I said trying to make light of it.

'Well it would get on my fucking nerves. He's your boyfriend, not your bodyguard.'

Her tone was sharp which was unusual for Rene. I remained silent, sipping my coffee, thinking I needed to take a couple of painkillers for the headache starting just above my left eyebrow. She tried to take the sting out of her words by patting my hand gently.

'Oh don't listen to me, silly old cow that I am, what the bloody hell do I know.'

She hauled herself up from the sofa with some effort and a sigh.

'Fancy a bacon sarnie?'

Mark joined us as soon as the smell of bacon had wafted up the stairs and woken him up.

'Morning gorgeous 'he said as he kissed the top of my head. 'Morning Rene, hows the head?'

'Banging 'she said. 'Now sit down while I get your breakfast.'

See, I wanted to say. See how nice he is to me, how nice he is to you. Don't think bad of him. He's a good guy.

We spent a lazy morning in our pj's, watching crap TV and eating chocolate. They insisted we stay for a late lunch although little persuasion was required when we saw the four rib of beef going in the oven. Over lunch the subject of our living arrangements came up.

'So why don't you two lovebirds live together full time then?'

It was a valid question asked by Gordon who looked first at Mark then at me, waiting for an answer. I too was waiting for an answer. All eyes were on Mark as he finished a mouthful of food.

'To be honest with you G, I'm a bit of a pain at times as I'm sure Cleo will testify.'

'Amen 'I said as I raised my wine glass. 'I'll drink to that.'

We all laughed including Mark. Was that hard for him to admit that or was he just playing the game? Did he cast his mind back to the last time he had lied in this very house about his son and the argument that had ensued?

'I've just had a thought 'Gordon said. 'A pal of mine has just bought a one bedroom flat in Sutton. He's giving it a lick of paint and whacking down some laminate flooring. He'll be looking for a tenant in the new year. How about I put in a good word for you and see if he'll give you a deal on the rent?'

Mark and I had discussed the possibility of him renting a flat on his own several times before. I thought it was extremely unhealthy for him to be living with his parents both mentally and physically. He was a forty one year old asthmatic man living part time in an attic where cigarette smoke wafted its way up the stairs and permeated his mattress, bedding and clothes. I knew he was hanging the situation out as long as possible in the hopes that I would relent and agree to him moving in full time. Considering I had told him that as long as there was a hole in my arse I wouldn't let that happen, he remained deluded and ever hopeful.

I quite liked the idea of Mark renting a flat, especially in Sutton which was only a fifteen minute drive from my house. I showed a lot more enthusiasm than Mark, asking Gordon if he could make the arrangements for us to view it as soon as possible. He promised he would call his pal the next day. I was well aware that Mark wasn't over the moon at the idea whereas I was doing cartwheels over it. If he had a place of his own albeit rented at least he would get off my back about moving in with me.

Thirteen

By February of 2005 Mark had moved in. The flat was on the ground floor of a rather large Edwardian house in a street situated in the nicer part of a not so nice town. Unfortunately it was the extended part of the house so lacked any original features or character. It was small with only three rooms. One bedroom, one bathroom minus a bath much to my dismay and an open plan kitchen and living area. It came furnished with cheap MDF wardrobes in a nasty shade of beech and a metal bed with a mattress that had about as much give as a slab of concrete. Two black faux leather sofas (make that armchairs) that were so small the manufacturer could have been done under the trades description act completed the look. I brought some things from my place to make it feel a bit more homely. A cashmere throw, framed photos of Mark and I, a couple of orchids and a buddha to watch over him.

One Saturday shortly after moving in Mark offered to cook us a three course meal from scratch while I was under strict instructions to sit back and do nothing. There was no argument from me. I had been feeling unusually tired in recent weeks and didn't have the energy or the inclination to help. The food he made was delicious. Dish after mouthwatering dish of calorific, high fat, artery clogging loveliness washed down with several glasses of crisp cold Sauvignon Blanc.

After clearing up he led me the one and a half steps it took to get from the kitchen area to the bedroom door. I gasped as he pushed it open. The room was covered in tea lights casting flickering shadows on the walls. On the bed which was scattered with rose petals was a big box tied with a very fancy ribbon from my favourite underwear shop.

'Oh Mark, it's beautiful, how lovely of you 'I said turning to give him a kiss.

He nodded towards the box. I pulled the ribbon off and lifted the lid to reveal a black fishnet bodysuit, the sort of underwear that demands raunchiness. Oh how I wished I had refused second helpings of the main course, not forgetting that third slice of chocolate torte. That had been pure gluttony. The last thing I wanted to do was step into a garment made out of weakly held together nylon, but Mark was looking at me so expectantly with that gleam in his eye that meant only one thing.

Leaving him lying on the bed I took myself and my stripper outfit to the bathroom to get changed. There was only a small mirror in there and for that I was grateful. I was busting out of the seams and looking down at my bloated belly I saw my flesh poking through the holes. How very attractive. Just as I was about to go back to the bedroom I realised I needed to pee and got into a right state trying to get the bloody thing off and on again. I took so long I thought he might have fallen asleep but no such luck. He was standing to attention and ready for action. After a tour round the flat stopping at every available surface that you could possibly shag on we fell into bed exhausted but satisfied. As Mark spooned me and cupped my breast in his hand he kissed my neck and mumbled sleepily.

'Your boobs feel huge. Goodnight babes, love you.'

And with that he was asleep. I on the other hand was now wide awake. He was right, my boobs had got bigger. Last week I had blamed Mark unfairly as it turned out for putting my bras on a hot wash. I tried on three and they were all very snug. Just the other night during sex I had told him to go easy on the nipple sucking as they had become very sensitive. Recent lack of energy, swollen boobs and sensitive nipples. I didn't like where this was heading.

Slipping out of bed I went to the bathroom and stood in front of the mirror for the second time that evening. Was it my imagination or did my nipples look darker? Was my belly bloated not due to my earlier feast but from a growing embryo. I was very bad at taking my birth control. I would pop a tablet from the blister pack, go to get a glass of water then get distracted. Two days later I would find the tablet on the window sill in the kitchen. When was my last period? The last one I could definitely remember was back in November. I had to cancel a spa day with a friend as it was so heavy. If that was the case I could be two or three months pregnant.

First thing tomorrow I would get a pregnancy test although it would be a waste of money. I was sure as eggs were ovulating eggs I was pregnant.

The next morning I offered to go and get the papers and some fresh bread while Mark was cooking sausages for our breakfast. In the local convenience store I found everything I needed including a pregnancy test. After reading the instructions and leaving the packaging in the glove compartment of my car I put the wand in my pocket. As soon as I got back I went to the bathroom and did what I had to do. It came as no surprise to see two lines appear indicating that I could have a baby if I so wished. The thought of telling Mark was making my stomach churn or was it the tiny life inside of me doing that? He would go ballistic, blaming me for my lack of responsibility regarding birth control. Wanting to get the conversation over and done with sooner rather than later I handed him the wand as he was turning the sausages in the frying pan.

'What you giving me a pen for? 'he asked with a puzzled expression on his face.

'It's not a pen, it's a pregnancy test.'

'Did you find it in the bathroom?'

'No Mark, I've just bought it. Please don't ask what for.'

He took it out of my hand and looked at it. His reaction

was not what I was expecting. A smile of delight as he picked me up, planted kisses all over my face exclaiming how wonderful it was. He must have seen from the look of near horror on my face that I didn't share his enthusiasm. I needed to bring him back to earth.

'Mark, please don't be ridiculous, I can't have a baby, I don't want a baby and I'm gobsmacked that you would even be considering it.'

He looked at me incredulously. 'Of course I want us to have a child together, why wouldn't I?'

'Er, because you don't have a lot to do with the one's you already have. You might not like admitting that you don't like responsibility but I don't have a problem owning up to it. Be honest with yourself Mark, you've run for the hills both times you've had kids. It would be the end of us if I had a baby and you know it.'

He insisted it wouldn't and pointed out that I was the only woman he had ever wanted to have children with, so it would be different with me.

Platitude after meaningless platitude tumbled from his mouth but I was having none of it.

'I'm having a termination and I don't want to hear anymore on the subject.'

Unfortunately I heard a lot more on the subject in the nine days leading up to it. He begged and pleaded with me not to go through with it. I couldn't understand where he was coming from. We could do what we liked when we liked without thought for anyone. We loved our city breaks and holidays in the sun. Eating out, day trips to the coast and spontaneous nights away in hotels. Call me selfish, but I was not prepared to give all that up and I was surprised that Mark was.

On the day of my appointment he drove me to the clinic and wandered around the local high street to wait for a few hours while I had a tube shoved between my legs to hoover away the unwanted guest in my womb. You would have thought I had undergone brain surgery, a triple heart bypass and a kidney transplant the way Mark carried on following my procedure. He drove me mad for days afterwards asking if I felt okay, was I in pain, telling me not to feel too guilty. Guilty? The only emotion I felt was pure relief that it was all over.

I'd not worked since we completed the Clapham flat and as nice as it was not having to rush out to work everyday I missed the routine and the satisfaction of earning money and getting a payslip each month. I decided to try and go back to work within the NHS but not in a clinical role. Stepping outside of my comfort zone I applied for the role of supervisor for the facilities department in a local mental health hospital. I got called for an interview and could not believe my luck when I walked into the office to meet Dan, my potential new boss. On his desk sat a Chelsea FC mug and on the wall behind a photo of him shaking hands with John Terry. I thought it best to get in quick and tell him I was a Chelsea girl born and bred and had spent a large part of my childhood and teenage years at Stamford Bridge. There ensued a fifteen minute conversation about his undying love for Chelsea and for Jose Mourinho who was indeed special in Dan's eyes. By the time the interview started I felt I had it in the bag already.

The role was to manage a team of fifteen craftsmen whose job it was to keep the hospital up and running. At the mention of fifteen men I thought to myself, Mark is going to go apeshit. Dan took me on a tour of the workshop and grounds and I had a good feeling about the place. Even as we heard screaming and foul language as we walked past the 136 suite which is where patients go when they are sectioned under the mental health act I felt comfortable. It was like a home from home. As I said goodbye to Dan he told me he still had three other candidates to interview but would let me know his decision by five thirty that day. I had to go home to wait for my future bosses's call on the landline. By five forty I was ringing Mark to tell him I'd got the job. He was over the moon, telling me what a clever girl I was and to get round to the flat where he had my favourite pink champagne on ice to celebrate my good news.

'So tell me all about it 'Mark said as we sipped our drinks.

I told him as much as I could about the role without divulging the fact that I would be working with men all day long. I was the only woman in the department and while that didn't bother me in the slightest I knew Mark would have something to say about it. I did however mention that my new boss seemed like a nice guy. Immediately his hackles were up.

'You only met him for half an hour, how do you know what he's like? 'he snapped.

'Okay, I got the impression he was a nice guy in the time I was with him 'I answered back.

He wanted to know more about him but there was nothing for me to tell.

'All I know for sure is that he's a Chelsea supporter.'

'Sounds like a prick if you ask me 'he sneered.

'I wasn't asking you, and if being a Chelsea fan makes him a prick what does that make you?'

I tried to inject a note of joviality into my voice to keep the conversation lighthearted. Mark had been a lifelong fan of the club so did that make him a prick I wondered.

By that point the celebratory mood had been broken and it appeared we were both looking for a fight. We continued to passively provoke each other for the next hour until unable to contain himself any longer Mark exploded and went for me as I was pouring myself another drink. He swiped the glass out of my hand sending it flying into the kitchen unit. I shoved him as hard as I could in the chest but he was as strong as an ox and didn't move an inch. He puffed up his chest and lifted his shoulders in a bid to intimidate me. I picked up a bread knife from the draining board in a bid to intimidate him.

'Go on 'he goaded through gritted teeth. 'Do it. Stab me and put me out of my misery.'

His words resonated with me and I immediately put the knife down. If I could relate to what he had just said did it mean that I too wanted to be put out of my misery?

One thing was certain. If we carried on the way we were one of us would surely get what we asked for.

Fourteen

I settled into my new job and loved every minute of it much to Mark's annoyance. He would enquire how my day at work had been and when I answered positively he would sneer and give me cut eye.

'Why do you bother asking me Mark, you're clearly not interested and it gives you the hump when I tell you I've enjoyed my day. Would you prefer it if I hated my job and was really miserable?'

'Of course not 'he answered having the good grace to look sorry.

For all his temper tantrums and outbursts of rage he did acknowledge in his saner moments that he was a 'complete cunt at times '(his words not mine, although I wholeheartedly agreed with him).

'It's just I know what blokes are like. The thought of them ogling you at work drives me crazy.'

'Surely not crazier than you are already 'I joked trying to keep the mood lighthearted.' Does it ever occur to you that within the group of men I work with the majority of them are very happily married or living with their partners? Of the two not in relationships, one is gay and the other is a seventeen-year-old apprentice.'

Trying to reason with Mark's extremely jealous personality was like pissing in the wind. Quite honestly I did not have a jealous bone in my body so it was difficult for me to empathise. If a woman looked at Mark when we were out I couldn't care less. Several women had flirted with him in front of me. Waitresses, trolley dollies on flights on our numerous trips abroad, shop assistant's, even a rather forward neighbour who actually told me outright she fancied him. And why not, he was rather fanciable. I was so cock sure of myself. Mark's at times atrocious behaviour towards me had left no chinks in my armour or dents in my pride. I was happy for other women to coo, tease and drool as much as they liked. He was coming home with me (most nights anyway).

In his warped mind he interpreted my lack of concern when another woman had an innocent flirt with him as not caring. I think he would have preferred me to confront the 'tart', and punch her lights out. Which is exactly what Mark did to a friend of his one Saturday evening after his paranoid thoughts got the better of him.

The day had started agreeably enough. We had gone over to see Mark's Mum and Dad and taken them out for lunch at their favourite restaurant which was a short walk from their house. We had good food and a couple of bottles of wine, consumed mainly by Paul and I as Mark was driving and Elaine's medication didn't mix well with alcohol. It was a lovely afternoon filled with stories from the good old days (Elaine's favourite subject) and lots of laughter. The four of us walked back in the sunshine feeling happy, full, relaxed and in the case of two of us, slightly tipsy. We stayed for coffee which Paul wanted to serve with brandy but I clocked Elaine's disapproving glare which Paul chose to ignore. I could see where this was heading so gave Mark a look that said we needed to skedaddle. He got the message and five minutes later we were on the doorstep saying our goodbyes. It was unusually warm for May and there was still heat in the sun even though it was late afternoon. Mark suggested a drink in the pub opposite Putney Common as we passed by on the way to the car.

I found us a table outside and enjoyed the atmosphere of the common, dog walkers, kids playing football, young girls lying on blankets reading magazines, the buzz of conversation from my fellow drinkers. Mark returned with my wine and his orange juice and lemonade. He sat next to me on the bench seat and put his arm around me, kissing me on the lips. I laid my head on his shoulder. It was a moment of utter tranquility and I'm grateful I enjoyed it however short it was.

The peace was shattered by the loud distinctive voice of Billy Big Nose (no prizes for guessing the origin of his nickname). He lolloped his way through the tables disturbing everyone's conversation.

'Mark, my man, whas appening? And Cleo, how come you get more beautiful every time I see you?'

Billy was an old friend of Mark's, his brain addled by too much alcohol and too many lines of cocaine. I would be lying if I said we were pleased to see him but there he was, attempting to squeeze his six foot five obese frame between the bench and the table opposite us. Finally wedged in, it would have been mean to expect him to get up and get a drink so Mark offered his services. I hoped he wouldn't take too long. Billy wasn't someone I had a lot in common with and I'm not sure I'd ever been in his company when he wasn't out of his nut. As he sat opposite me, constantly sniffing and wiping his nose with the back of his hand I forced myself to look interested as he waffled on about nothing in particular. I looked back over my shoulder and was relieved to see Mark walking towards the table. I mouthed 'Thank God 'but Mark was looking past me staring hard at Billy. I was familiar with the expression on his face. It was so easy to read. Trouble was imminent. I had no time to even consider what or who had set him off. As he reached the table, the pint was slammed down, most of its contents sloshing out of the glass.

'Whoa 'shouted Billy. 'What's your problem?'

Mark's swift answer came in the form of a punch straight to the side of Billy's head. I could not believe my eyes. I was speechless. Poor old Billy was also speechless but for a different reason. He was sparko, his sizeable head slumped forward resting on his chest.

'What the fu...'

Before I had a chance to finish my sentence Mark was going for him again. By now I was on my feet on Billy's side of the table trying in vain to protect him from another punch raining down on him.

'Move out the way Cleo, I mean it. I'm gonna fucking hurt the cunt.'

He pushed me aside and grabbed a now dazed and confused Billy round the neck. Mark leaned in close to his friends face and spoke with laboured breath.

'If I ever catch you looking down Cleo's top again I will rip your dirty fucking balls off.'

Billy's attempt at an answer was drowned out by me shouting rather loudly' What the hell are you going on about?'

I looked down at my chest half expecting to see a boob hanging out of my bra or an escaped nipple on show. I actually laughed, a slightly hysterical version of my normal laughter it has to be said. There was nothing remotely funny about the scene unfolding before me.

Suddenly all Mark's attention was on me, allowing Billy to make a run for it. He wasn't going to struggle to get up as he had struggled to get in. There was a sound of splintering wood as the slatted table top split in two due to the force of Billy's forearms pushing up from underneath. With space to move he was up and running, and I do mean running. Amazing what a bit of adrenaline can do. When it kicks in it gives you the choice of fight or flight, defend or flee. Billy had chosen well, taking the flight and flee options.

All around us people had started moving away from our table calling out for kids and dogs to return to their respective owners. I had a feeling that one of them had probably called the police. Not the most streetwise clientele in that area of Putney. Had we been in a pub in another part of the borough customers would have classed it as the evening entertainment.

'Keep away from me Mark 'I said in no uncertain terms as I began walking towards the pavement not sure whether to head towards the train station or in the opposite direction to the bus stop.

Mark was in a dilemma, chase after Billy and finish what he started or move onto his next victim which happened to be me and start a new fight. As soon as he opened his mouth to speak I did something incredibly childish and incredibly satisfying. I stuck my fingers in my ears and began singing "Ruby Don't Take Your Love To Town". I had no idea what prompted my song choice, but I used to listen to Kenny Rogers with my mum when I was growing up and knew every word to nearly every song. I couldn't listen to another word from him. My singing drowned out his voice but he was walking close behind me furiously pulling on my biceps trying to get my arms down. Of course he was stronger than me but he wasn't faster than me. As we came onto the main road I decided I was going to make a run for it down the next side street which was about ten yards away. I cursed myself for busting out the flip flops from the back of my wardrobe that morning. If it hadn't been so sunny I would have had my Converse on. I quickened my step as a hopeless warm up and as soon as I reached the corner I was off. Not exactly Flo-Jo more like Slow-Mo bearing in mind I was wearing inappropriate footwear and had a belly full of food and wine. All that mattered was that I was faster than Norman Bates. I lost him somewhere between The Jolly Gardners pub and the high street. I slowed my pace but daren't come to a stop. I decided to make my way to the train station so as not to risk being spotted waiting at a bus stop. Great minds think alike or rather in mine and Norm's case fools never differ. As I turned the corner there he was pacing up and down outside the station. How the hell did he get there before me I asked myself. A change of plan was called for. I would call a minicab. Easier said than done. I had no mobile and there was no phone booth in sight.

As I pondered alternative journey options I kept my eyes glued on Mark (never lose sight of the enemy and all that). I wasn't close enough to hear his phone ring but it must have done. He answered and by the look of his body language the conversation was far from jovial. He was still looking around but was obviously concentrating on his phone call. I had a feeling it was Billy Big Nose (or should I say Billy even bigger nose after Mark's punch). His voice was rising, I could tell from the way passers by were doing a double take as they walked past him. After another minute or so he moved away from the station entrance and stood in the doorway of a shop that had closed down.

I made my move. The lights were red allowing pedestrians to cross safely. I bolted across the road and hurried head down towards the station, fumbling in my bag as I walked quickly to the entrance, my fingers coming across a loose five pound note. Luck was on my side, no queue at the ticket office and an efficient London Underground employee who fired off my ticket in seconds. I was through the barrier and on the way down the stairs when I heard my name bellowing out behind me. It was pointless looking back. I would have wasted precious seconds confirming what I already knew. I needed to concentrate on getting on the train that was waiting on the platform. I heard the guard blow his whistle and realised I had several steps and the width of the platform between me and a safe place. Reverting back to my childhood days, fearless and slightly reckless I jumped the remaining steps to the bottom twisting my ankle on landing and losing my left flip flop. There was no time to retrieve it as the doors began to close. I launched myself through the rapidly decreasing gap, stumbling onto the train which to my relief was quite empty. I had no idea where it was going, but it was moving away from him and that was all that mattered.

The moment my arse hit the nearest seat the feeling of relief that washed over me brought tears to my eyes. In an effort to keep the tears from actually spilling over and falling down my face I closed them and bowed my head down. The momentum of the train calmed me and a voice inside my head began a chant in rhythm with the click clack sound of the train moving along the tracks.

'I fucking hate him, I fucking hate him, I fucking hate him. ' A child's voice interrupted my mantra.

'Mama, why has that lady only got one shoe on?'

I kept my head down and despite my mood, was curious to hear the answer. The mothers voice. foreign, soft and husky, spoke gently to her child.

'Sshh Celine, maybe the lady lost it and is going shopping to get a new pair. Now, show me your book and we'll read together.'

When I raised my head a moment later I looked opposite me straight into the eyes of Celine who whilst pretending to listen to her mother was clearly more interested in me. She was a pretty girl of about five or six with long dark hair and chubby cheeks with a body to match. The sort of cute kid you could cuddle and eat at the same time. I gave her a little smile and a wink before rooting around in my bag for a tissue.

'Mama, why has that lady been crying?'

This time the mother's voice was a little harsher.

'Oh Celine, it's rude to stare and ask such questions.'

'It's okay 'I said. 'It's right for children to be inquisitive isn't it?'

I said to the little girl.' I'll tell you what happened shall I? My shoe fell off and because I was in a bit of a rush I didn't have time to pick it up and I'm a bit sad because I had a row with my friend.'

'Why did you row with your friend? 'she asked.

'Well', I explained 'sometimes my friend can be a bit

naughty and say unkind things.'

Her mouth fell open in astonishment and her eyes grew wide.

'Is your friend called Charlotte?'

'No 'I answered.

'Well, my friend is called Charlotte and sometimes she's horrible to me and calls me fatty.'

Oh, bless this kid I thought, tears threatening again. Before I had a chance to answer she went on.

'My teacher, Miss Harrison says I should keep away from Charlotte and find someone else to play with.'

'That's a good idea, I'm sure there's lots of children in your class. 'I said.

She pondered this for a moment before saying 'But I just wanna be friends with Charlotte cos when she's not being mean she's really really nice.'

Snap, I thought. I know somebody just like that. The world could be a cruel place, especially where children were concerned. I could stick up for myself, fight my corner and be just as nasty back when Mark started on me but it was different for kids. Waving goodbye to the little girl as she left the train at the next stop, I hoped she would toughen up and tell Charlotte to go fuck herself whilst poking her in the eye with a pencil.

Alas, the solution to my problems was not quite so easy.

After Mark's ridiculous outburst all in the name of protecting my tits, I realised that even though I was fully aware he had anger issues I hadn't taken them seriously enough. They felt very serious at the time but when things blew over as they always did, I tended to look back and convince myself that it wasn't so bad. Much easier to dilute the memory, pouring water on it, easier to digest if the images got weaker. I wasn't a stupid girl even though you could be forgiven for thinking I was educationally sub normal for putting up with all the crap that Mark brought to my life.

Needless to say he was mortified with his behaviour, he was so sorry, he was going to make it up to me....... yadda yadda yadda.

I told him to shut up. This time I was going to tell him what was going to happen.

'You are going to make an appointment with your GP explaining that you have serious problems managing your anger and that you need help as you are a danger to those around you.'

He looked slightly shocked but admitted defeat.

'Okay, okay. I know you're right, I need to sort myself out, but will you come with me?'

'I actually think it will be better for you to go alone 'I answered gently 'and', I continued 'a lot of your problems seem to stem from me. I appear to be the instigator of the majority of your rages. You might want to get things off your chest that you don't want me to hear.'

'Cleo', he declared, 'YOU are my fucking saviour. You are absolutely not the problem. It's all me, but If you think I'm bad now, I can't imagine what I would be like if you left me. I'll only go if you come with me.'

I wasn't happy about it but if it meant he was getting help I could hardly say no.

Aside from his extreme anger and absurd jealousy he had also began to show signs of OCD. I first noticed it one day in the supermarket. As we strolled through the fruit and veg section he said he wanted grapes. He put a container of every single grape variety they had for sale in the trolley which totalled eight cartons 'Slightly excessive wouldn't you say? 'I asked smiling and looking more than a little puzzled. He insisted he wanted them all. I asked him to choose some olives while I went to get some salad dressing. On my return not a minute later I came back to find ten jars of olives in the trolley.

'Jesus Mark, we don't need that many 'I half laughed reaching in to remove some.

'No, leave them please 'he insisted. 'I can't decide which ones I want so I'll take them all.'

I put my foot down in the bakery section where he attempted to put five freshly baked French sticks, a cranberry and nut loaf and four packets of burger buns in the trolley.

'We haven't even got bread on the shopping list. We've got plenty indoors, the French sticks go stale in about six hours, the nuts get stuck in your teeth and we've got no fucking burgers to put in the fucking buns...'

I took a deep breath and silently urged myself to calm down. We negotiated and ended up going home with one French stick that went rock hard in five hours in fact, ending up untouched in the bin. It was the same with clothes shopping. He would find something he liked and refuse to try it on convincing himself it would fit purely because he wanted it to. He would buy four in exactly the same colour to be hung in his wardrobe never to see the light of day again.

His compulsions were applied to the oddest items. One morning he woke up in bed at my house declaring the rather expensive Siberian goose down pillows he had been sleeping on for the past year unsuitable. Apparently they were making his already painful neck ache even more. His rugby playing days had caused a hump to form at the top of his spine affecting his neck and the nerves running down his left arm leaving him with constant pins and needles in his fingers and nerve pain. He was waiting to hear from the hospital with a date for surgery. Over the next three weeks he made it his mission to track down his perfect pillow. He tried to rope me into his shopping expeditions but I refused on the grounds of having better things to do. The first two he came home with and slept on overnight were deemed useless.

'Soft as shit 'were his exact words.

Of course the pillows couldn't be returned due to hygiene reasons. The second set were too hard.

'Like resting my head on a couple of breeze blocks'.

The third set smelt like old socks. And so it went on until we were in possession of eighteen once used then discarded pillows. He had been dumping them in my spare room as there was no room in his flat. They were blocking the access to my wardrobe. By the Saturday of the third week my patience was wearing so thin it was anorexic. When Mark suggested lunch out and a stroll down the Kings Road in Chelsea I was happy to agree. Unfortunately he ruined the gesture my mentioning as an after thought that he wanted to pop into Peter Jones, the department store overlooking Sloane Square to check out their bedding department.

I lost the plot, marching up the stairs to the spare room throwing all the pillows one after the other down the stairs until it looked as if a giant marshmallow had invaded the house. I was screaming and shouting, using very foul language calling him every offensive name I could associate with being wacko as I could think of. I told him I wanted them out of the house.

'But what am I going to do with them? 'he asked, bewildered by both my actions and the thought of where he was going to take them.

'I couldn't give a monkeys what you do with them, take them to the charity shop, drop them into a homeless shelter, sell them at a boot fair, just get them the fuck out of here.'

I watched him from the front room window as he stuffed the pillows into his car, filling the boot then the back seat. He came back a couple of hours later with a massive bouquet of flowers and a bottle of Sancerre by way of an apology.

His obsessions touched every area of our lives in one form or another. I bought a honey and mustard dip from Marks and Spencers to accompany some chicken and jacket potatoes that we had for a mid week dinner. He loved the dip. I mean really loved it. So much so that he wanted it with every dinner I cooked from thereon in. From chicken satay and stir fry veg to beef wellington, beans on toast, calves liver and bacon, fish and chips and spag bol. I bought tubs of the stuff until disaster struck and my local M&S stopped stocking it.

One night I cooked a leek and mushroom risotto with crusty bread and served it up with a crisp salad and a glass of ice cold chardonnay each. After commenting on how delicious the meal looked he asked where the dip was. I explained they weren't stocking it in our local store anymore. He actually called the custom care department to complain. The young lady he spoke to assured him it had only been discontinued in certain stores and he could still find it in their flagship store in Oxford Street. Guess where we went the next day. Travelling sixteen miles on a dirty old train to a street packed with tourists and pick pockets was not my idea of fun on my day off from work. Nor was it Mark's, and I could tell he was regretting his decision by the way he was bumping through the crowds telling people to get out of his way. To add insult to injury after scouring the deli section for the holy grail of dips we were told by a very sweet shop assistant

'Oh, I'm, sorry, we've stopped stocking that as it wasn't very popular. Have you tried the minted pea and basil, it's lovely with scampi.'

He mowed the lawn in a certain pattern, un-fortunately not straight lines, threw one of my orchids in the bin because according to him the flowers weren't pointing in the right direction. He couldn't sleep until he had rubbed up and down my back seven times and told me he loved me. I asked him what he did when he wasn't with me and he told me he rubbed his arm and said I love you in his head.

So, off we went to the GP with a shitload of nuttiness to

describe in the hopes they could help him. His GP prescribed him with tablets that numbed his senses and emotions. Mark said it felt like he was walking on sponges and his mouth was full of cotton wool. Apparently they were side effects that wore off after the first couple of weeks. We never got the opportunity to see if they did wear off as a letter arrived giving him a date for his neck operation. Mark in his wisdom decided to cease the medication which the GP had strongly advised him not to do. Maybe he thought that while they were sorting out his neck they could straighten out the wires to his brain. If only.

Fifteen

To say Mark was a difficult patient would be akin to saying Hitler was a bit of a bad egg. We both knew from what the consultant had explained that it was going to be a long and painful recovery following his neck surgery. I didn't realise that applied to me as well.

From the second he left the bed in the hospital to go home following his operation he was an arsehole. We had a screaming match in the car before we had even left the hospital grounds with him accusing me of putting the passenger seat in the wrong position. If you've ever tried assisting a twenty two stone, six foot one man with a fused neck and a face like a wet weekend into a Porsche Boxter you would have felt my pain, if you haven't, take my word for it, it was hell. If it was bad getting him in, getting him out was a hundred times worse. We had decided to stay at his flat as it was on one level so navigating stairs would be one less thing to worry about. For the first few days he could hardly move and it was left to me to do very nearly everything for him. He could clean his teeth but couldn't spray deodorant under his arms. He could stand in the shower but couldn't wash himself. He could sit on the toilet but couldn't wipe his arse. He could sit on the sofa but couldn't get up. He could get an erection but couldn't have sex. So I got left with spraying deodorant, washing his balls, wiping his arse, hurting my back pulling him up from the sofa and keeping him distracted when he felt horny. Progress was slow but by the end of the first week he was finding it easier to move about. I had taken two weeks off work and I happened to mention that if he continued to improve he would be okay to be left on his own when I went back.

'Suppose you're missing the lads are you? Missing making them cups of tea and taking them in homemade biscuits?'

His voice was pure venom and I looked at him thinking what a nasty piece of work he was.

'Actually Mark, they make me tea. John, the carpenter brings me in a chocolate croissant every Friday and Boyce the plumber brings me a packet of pear drops every week.'

I was tempted to add 'and I give them both a big kiss and cuddle for their kindness 'but by the look on his face I thought that might just send him over the edge.

Even being in so much pain didn't deter him from his jealous thoughts. It was going to be a tough few weeks ahead. In fact it ended up being a tough few months both physically and mentally. Mark did not like being out of work. Especially now that he was paying rent and bills that were significantly higher than when he was at his mum and dads. He was self employed so, no work equaled no pay. He continued to drop hints about how it made more sense to be living together. I was brought up to be financially savvy and of course I agreed with him but the difference was I didn't need financial help, thank you very much. I had no mortgage and my bills were covered by my salary with more than a few bob left to spare. Even so, it was always Mark that spent the most money out of the two of us. He continued to display unstinting generosity, lavishing me with underwear, jewellery and nights out in expensive restaurants which quite honestly I could have done without.

One Sunday in early November as we relaxed over breakfast reading the papers I spotted a competition in one of the supplements that caught my attention. It was run in conjunction with a celebrity hairdresser whose adverts were all over the television. Readers were asked to send in a picture of themselves accompanied by a few lines explaining why they thought they deserved a hair make over and an all expenses trip for two, to New York with five hundred pounds spending money.

Out came the digital camera (the same one that had caused so much aggro in Iceland). Mark took a few head shots of me with my long, unbrushed, five day unwashed hair and printed them off. I sent the worse photo in with one word to accompany the image "HELP".

I posted it the next day and completely forgot about it.

Preparations for Christmas started in late November and the usual running around like a headless chicken continued until the twenty fourth of December. My rule has always been if it ain't done by midday on Christmas Eve it ain't happening.

Christmas came and went in a haze of food, alcohol, and for the most part peace and joy. Just as the January blues were setting in I answered the phone to a very jolly girl who introduced herself as Isobel from the Sunday Telegraph. She was delighted to inform me that I had won the hair make over competition and was I available to travel in February. I confirmed that was fine and she took down some details. When she asked who would be accompanying me I had to think for a moment. Mark's name should have rolled off my tongue but instead it was getting caught in my throat. I so wanted to say Lisa. My dear friend who was always there for me, always supportive, never judgemental. What fun we would have, swanning up and down Fifth Ave, buying knock off gear in Canal Street, eating pizzas and drinking Peroni in Little Italy. There was no point in day dreaming about the fun I could have had with my mate. Mark would have been very upset to think I would have chosen Lisa over him.

The jolly Isobel asked if there was anything she could arrange for us to do in NYC.

'Obviously Darling, you'll have to spend a day getting your hair done, having some pics taken for the article and all that malarkey but after that the worlds your oyster or at least New York is. Now, how about a broadway show on one of the nights?'

She mentioned some titles but nothing really took my fancy.

'Okay let's see if there's any sporting events, maybe something at Madison Square Garden. I don't suppose you like Billy Joel do you?'

At which point I had to stop myself screaming with delight.

'Like him? I absolutely love him.'

He was actually one of our favourite singers and we'd seen him in concert a couple of times before. When I told Mark about winning the competition and seeing Billy J at Madison Square Garden he was so excited. I felt bad about my initial thoughts of not wanting to be with him. The truth was, when he was stable we always had enormous fun together and I began to look forward to our trip.

The second month of 2006 was soon upon us and as we boarded the plane to NYC I hoped Mark's recent good mood would continue stateside. He had been particularly loving in recent weeks and life was bobbing along nicely. I had been to New York a couple of times before and of course Mark had got married there in 1997 to his second wife. We were there for five nights/six days and apart from a day spent in a very upmarket salon on Fifth Ave having my tresses chopped, coloured and tamed and my face painted for a photo shoot we were able to do our own thing.

We were proper tourists and even though we'd both been up the Empire State Building before we hadn't been together. I had a horrible feeling that Mark was going to propose at the top of it. It had been about three months since he had last asked me which was quite a long gap for him. He didn't ask but if he did it would have been my usual no. Far too cold up there to take my hands out of my pockets.

We shopped for England, buying so much stuff we had to buy a cheap holdall to put it all in. Billy Joel was on point, creating an amazing atmosphere, giving us both a night we would never forget. Unfortunately the last night was also memorable but for all the wrong reasons.

We had eaten a fantastic burger in a place recommended to us by our bellboy at the hotel. The cocktails were going down a treat as we toasted my hair and thanked its lack of style and bad condition for getting us here. We had another potent cocktail to toast my new "do" which had been cut to my shoulders with choppy layers and bleached so blonde it was practically white. I loved it. Mark loved it. We were laughing and enjoying ourselves. Silly me, I was with Mark so I should have known it wouldn't last. We walked hand in hand back to the hotel with one thing on our mind. Mark and I were so well matched when it came to sex. We made love often. It was the most settled part of our relationship. Adventurous, active, loving and healthy. It was the only time I could guarantee Mark would behave appropriately.

As we walked near Central Park I asked Mark jokingly if he had ever shagged someone on a horse and carriage ride, and if he hadn't would he like to.

Obviously I was joking. In an instant I knew I had said the wrong thing. He tightened his grip on my hand, his casual stroll of the moment before now a determined stride pulling me along with him.

'You've done it already haven't you? You've fucked someone on a carriage ride over there 'he growled pointing across the avenue to the park.

'Come on Mark, as if. Nobody in their right mind would do that. You'd be arrested for public lewdness or some such charge.'

There was no talking him round. He had it in his head that I had committed a sexual act with I don't know who in a carriage whilst being pulled along by a horse being driven by an extra from the Sopranos. The tone was set for the remainder of our last evening. Walking in silence back to our hotel I thought how sad it was that such a fantastic trip was spoilt at the last moment. Another thought struck me. It wasn't the first time this had happened.

We went away a lot, long weekend European city breaks, last minute four day beach holidays, a week or two in a villa in Italy or Spain, trips to the states and the Caribbean. We would have a blinding time until the last day or night when gradually his mood would deteriorate and almost invariably the trip would end on a bad note. So true to form another shit end to a great holiday.

I was expecting a very quiet hotel room that night with only Fox news or CNN in the background for company as I packed (or rather, crammed) our cases but the man surprised me. He wanted to talk. Unfortunately for him our moods did not coincide and I was absolutely not in the mood for talking, especially when I heard the subject matter. His favourite topic. Me and other men. In my head I was repeating over and over 'please fuck off and stop boring the knickers off of me'.

My reactions and behaviour regarding Mark's moods and accusations varied vastly depending on my own mood at the time. I had gone from deliriously happy to extremely pissed off in a matter of minutes. As I pottered about the hotel room practising my deep breathing, trying to ignore Mark's voice I knew the evening was going to end badly. I wasn't giving him the reaction he was looking for and quite frankly once I knew everything had gone to shit a tiny part of me thought 'bring it on'.

As I pointed out before I was no Mother Teresa and at times I was the one who lashed out first. I could say 'It wasn't my fault, he drove me to it 'but I won't. I'll be honest and say there were times when I wanted to hurt him of my own accord without any provocation from him. His voice was going through me, going on and on and on about this bloke and that bloke. About the time he caught our neighbour spying on me in my bikini while I was sunbathing in the garden. About the electrician at work who had bought me flowers as a thank you after I had made his daughter a Barbie cake. I couldn't take it a moment longer. I was behind him as I picked up the mini bar's cork screw from the table next to where he was sitting and walloped him on the back of his head with it.

'SHUT THE FUCK UP 'I shouted and he did for about two seconds before he retaliated. He must have been slightly dazed as he got to his feet swaying slightly before he stumbled into me with the full force of his weight and I fell face first onto the large wooden paddle shaped arm of the chair. It caught me spot on my brow bone and to add insult to injury or rather injury to injury I bit down on my bottom lip so hard I felt the blood dripping off my chin.

In an instant he was trying to help me up, offering me loo roll to wipe my chin. Saying sorry over and over again. Ordering ice from room service, wrapping it in a flannel and holding it to my eye which appeared to be swelling up by the minute. Honestly he would have put Florence Nightingale to shame.

We lay next to each other on the bed sipping brandy straight from the little bottles from the minibar. If it was supposed to help with shock it wasn't working. I was finding it very hard to accept that I would be arriving back in dear old Blighty with a black eye, a fat lip and a head of hair straight out of a Hollywood film set.

Sixteen

To say that life carried on as normal would be one way of putting it.

But whose to say what's normal. What may be run of the mill to some folks could be totally out there to others. A remarkable event to one person may be an everyday occurrence to another.

The life that had become the norm to me carried on. When it was good it was very very good and when it was bad it was horrid (a bit like the little girl who had a little curl right in the middle of her forehead).

Looking back over the years my recall of events becomes somewhat hazy from that point on. I know what happened just not in the exact chronological order. This lack of recall could be due to the copious amount of alcohol I had started to consume at that time. Alternatively it could be my sub conscious protecting me from memories best forgotten.

Taking this into consideration I will endeavour to document the significant events that led me up to the point when a huge amount of crap hit a very large fan and created one hell of a mess.

We continued to divide our time between Mark's flat and my house though not equally. My house was nicer, had a staircase and lacked damp patches so we spent the majority of our time there. I was well aware that our living arrangements did not make financial sense but the thought of commitment in any shape or form scared me more than it did Mark. As a compromise we thought about buying a holiday home together. In the summer of 2006 we looked into buying a place on the Isle of Wight but decided the novelty of spending time on an island stuck in a time warp might wear off.

We attended Mark's brothers wedding in Bournemouth where I was wrongly accused of sneaking out of the hotel with a fellow guest the night before the wedding to have sex on the lawn. Risking my own and other peoples lives I drove the one hundred miles home, very drunk, very upset, at two in the morning. Answered the home phone at 5am to hear Mark pleading with me to come back otherwise he wouldn't go to the wedding. I called a cab to take me back. A lovely time was had by all.

Took up sketching and painting which really helped me switch off and relax.

I went on what was supposedly an all girls trip to Spain. Mark clearly didn't get the memo. He was spotted mooching about outside the hotel we were in. When I confronted him with stalking me he claimed he was there to surprise me. What a lovely surprise (not).

We decorated the house and landscaped the garden.

I had regular marriage proposals from Mark which all ended with the same answer.

Thought my bras had been on a hot wash again. Swollen boobs, sore nipples and an unopened box of tampons in the bathroom cabinet led me to the awful conclusion that I was pregnant again. Telling Mark I was having a week away with Lisa at a health farm I booked myself an appointment at a clinic in London for my second and last termination. I told Mark I wasn't happy taking the pill anymore and asked him if he would consider a vasectomy.

'Let me put it like this 'I said. 'Do you want to marry me?'

'Of course 'came the answer.

'I don't want children 'I said 'so if we get married the only baby you would be having would be with someone else and that would make it illegitimate. You've got one illegitimate son already, were you thinking of having another one?'

Four weeks later her was booked in for the procedure.

The most painful part for Mark was the thought that he

may have to abstain from sex for two weeks. As it turned out the incision was no longer than a centimetre and his swollen balls went down quickly. Within nine days he was back to normal minus the ability to father anymore children. (every cloud). Twelve weeks after that sperm from a wank into a specimen pot was tested confirming he was firing blanks.

In June of 2007 we spent four weeks apart when Mark got a job working in Spain.

Missed him, missed him not, missed him, missed him not. Life was always that bit easier when he wasn't around. His attempts to control me from a distance were pathetic. Telling me to make sure I was home every night so he could call me on the home phone.

Our reunions were always joyful. I often felt Mark had a fresh sense of determination to change his ways following time apart from each other. Then I would chastise myself for being so naive as he continued to display Othello like levels of jealousy ranging from the absurd to the ridiculous. Not satisfied with accusing me of assignation's with other men he got it into his head that I was also seeing other women. Added to my supposed flirting and carrying on with my male colleagues I'm amazed I had the energy left for anything else. I took great pleasure in telling him that our works Christmas party had been booked. It was a no partners event as it was being paid for by the department. He wound himself up from the moment I told him about it. He could not cope with the fact that I would be the only woman amongst sixteen men and alcohol would be involved.

The police were called when he turned up uninvited and brimming with testosterone at the hotel where the event was taking place. Unfortunately for everyone involved he picked the moment I was sitting on the dance floor in a line of people performing 'Oops upside your head 'with my legs straddling Dan, my boss.

Trying to cave my bosses head in did little for my chances of promotion but luckily for Mark, Dan was a better man than he was and dropped all charges. I had to concur with Donna Summer and Barbra Streisand, that sometimes 'enough is enough'. It really was bad timing being the season of goodwill and all that but I couldn't put it off any longer. I told him it was over (again). Told him I meant it (again).

In my haste to terminate our relationship I forgot some rather important items that needed to be retrieved from the flat including:

Two pairs of Prada sunglasses

Passport

Buddha

Limited edition Converse hi tops

Large wad of rolled up fifty pound notes stashed inside hi tops

Cashmere hot water bottle

Drawer full of sexy underwear (shame to waste it)

I really could not face going round there so I sent my dear friend Lisa to do my dirty work. Three failed attempts before the nosy old bird next door informed her she saw Mark and a short fat bloke moving gear out. That short fat bloke was his brother John. I was sure of it.

The very next day I'm banging on a door in Putney expecting a warm welcome from Elaine. (Note to self - lower expectations). Bypassing the small talk I launched straight in and asked where the arsehole was.

In Sweden it turned out.

'He's gone to see his son 'she said as if that was the answer I should have been expecting. 'About time too 'she added defiantly as if I was the one who had stopped him going before now.

Her answer was somewhat of a shock but not an altogether unpleasant one. I had got the answer I came for and was keen to get out of that bad vibe house. I held back from singing George Michael's 'Freedom 'on the way out and waited till I was clear of the front garden and on the main road.

Eight days of heaven followed. I unplugged the home phone and told my girlfriends if they received any communication from Mark whatsoever, not to answer his calls or reply to texts. They assured me they wouldn't.

I went out drinking, dancing, flirting, fancying until a call to my work phone from Sweden on day nine put a stop to that.

Tears, apologies, promises and pleading from Mark to try again. He missed me, couldn't live without me, he loved me so much, he would get help............

I was steadfast in my answers, telling him to stay put and spend time with his boy but in true Mark and Cleo fashion by the fifth phone call he had worn me down. I picked him up from Heathrow a week later. We didn't even make it home that night. We got as far as the first airport hotel where we checked in and went to the bar. I don't think either of us were in the mood for a deep and meaningful conversation, more interested in getting each others clothes off and falling into bed. We needed to talk but it could wait for another time. When we did talk I pointed out that there was no reason for him to be so secretive about his son in Sweden. I suggested we take a trip there so I could meet him. Mark agreed but after me mentioning it a few times I got the vibes that he wasn't keen and as it wasn't high on my to do list I gave up asking.

We bought a caravan in Marlow on the River Thames which was close enough to London that we could commute to work. I'm happy to say we spent a lot of mostly peaceful times there. We made it like a home from home, laying wooden floors, upholstering the sofa's and building a large veranda where we spent hot summers, cosy autumns and happy days. Our caravan days were cut short following a spectacular row after psycho accused me of flirting with the man next door to us. A seventy year old overweight balding man who walked with a stick and wore socks with his sandals. After a screaming match on our veranda which was great entertainment for our neighbours he locked me in the caravan (for my own safety apparently) and drove into town to get some shopping. I climbed out of a window, unfortunately landing on a spotlight smashing it and getting a shard of glass embedded in my leg. A visit to AE and four stitches later I told him to sell the caravan.

He was a ruiner of all things good.

Joe at work taught me how to play guitar. I spent nearly every lunchtime for three months strumming and picking until I had mastered one of my all time favourite songs 'Whats going on 'by 4 non blondes. It's my party piece when Mark's not at the party. I could never tell him I had been under the tutelage of another man so the guitar I bought for myself had to remain at work. To this day he still doesn't know I can play.

We continued taking our trips abroad including a walking holiday to Austria where thanks to Mark's map reading we veered off the beaten track and got lost up a mountain. The hotel were five minutes short of sending out a search party for us.

We spent my big four 0 knocking back Dirty Martinis at the black jack tables in Vegas.

Happy to walk (or should I say stagger) away with three thousand dollars.

Mark busted out the Cartier again, presenting me with a insanely expensive but beautiful watch.

I took up knitting and jewellery making.

Learning to live with Mark's absurd obsessions never got any easier. The juice preoccupation is one that sticks in my mind. Literally overnight he discovered a taste for fruit juice that would only be satisfied if the fridge contained eleven cartons of juice. No more, no less. They could be different flavours or all the same but there had to be eleven cartons on the nose. I refused to participate in encouraging such behaviour and told him I was happy to buy two at the most. He would buy the other nine and then try to cram them into an already stuffed fridge. He would stand in front of it letting all the cold air out counting and recounting the cartons sometimes for five minutes until whatever it was in his brain clicked and he was able to close the door.

The shutters at my windows had to be set at a particular angle and he checked them several times a day to make sure they hadn't moved.

Wear marks were starting to show in different parts of the house where he had to touch certain things as he walked past. At the bottom of the stairs he had to turn around in a circle before he could carry on walking.

A friend of mine who was studying clinical psychology spent a weekend with us and on the Monday evening she called to say two things. Firstly - thanks for a lovely weekend, and secondly - why hadn't I ever mentioned that Mark had OCD/autistic tendencies?

Mark took Harry to France on a boys only trip which I was more than happy for them to go on. I felt it was important that they spent time together on their own.

It came to light that Mark had got himself into serious debt spread over several credit cards. I could have helped him out but I chose not to. Credit where it's due, he made a huge effort to curb his spending and pay them off and within a year he was debt free.

Slaps, kicks and punches remained a very small part of our lives. Mark was on the receiving end more than I was.

I swam five days a week.

In the changing room one morning I caught one of the regulars eyeing up a bruise on my upper arm

'Yeah, I had a fight with my partner three days ago but don't worry his bruise is bigger.'

I continued escaping from his clutches whenever I felt the need going on yoga retreats and spa weekends with my health conscious girlfriends. Then it was Dubai or Abu Dhabi with my girls that liked to party. I stayed strong lifting weights and doing two hundred sit ups a day convincing myself that it would make up for the amount I was drinking. I even started smoking which Mark hated with a vengeance giving me all the more reason to carry on just to wind him up.

We went on a five week tour of Europe which was very exciting despite the disagreement we had regarding the route. I wanted to include Northern Europe particularly Norway and Sweden. Mark was reluctant. We settled on driving through France into Spain and Portugal ending up in Morocco where I lost ten pounds in four days due to a very tasty but dodgy chicken tagine.

Returning home after being away always seemed to unsettle me and our return from Europe was no different. I felt like I had got stuck in a rut at work. It was a nice happy environment, I got on with everybody and we always had a laugh. Considering Mark's behaviour towards my boss that Christmas I was lucky to have the job at all. The role was just not challenging enough and I could feel my brain cells dying slowly due to lack of stimulation. On second thoughts my brain cells might have been dying due to the amount of alcohol I was knocking back. I decided to go back to a clinical role and got a job taking blood donations from donors on a team that travelled to a different location everyday. I'm happy to say it was and remains to this day the best job ever. Knowing I have played a part in saving or improving a persons quality of life gives great job satisfaction.

We celebrated Elaine and Paul's fifty years of wedded bliss in October 2012 with three nights on the Isle of Wight.

We spent a lot of time with our dear friends Rene and Gordon and over the years it had become a tradition to spend Christmas with them. Mark broke with it one year to spend Christmas with his Ma, Pa and his son Harry. I was invited but Mark knew my answer before he even asked the question.

'Would love to Mark but unfortunately I'll be busy sipping Dom Perignon and nibbling on foie gras before tucking into a 25lb turkey with all the trimmings followed by opening presents from classy shops taken from under a beautifully decorated ten foot Christmas tree.'

I dressed to impress. Low cut backless black dress with killer heels and my hair up with long dangling earrings touching my collarbone. He drove over on Christmas morning to kiss me under the mistletoe.

'Fucking hell, you look stunning 'he said glumly when he saw me.

'Don't look so upset about it. It's better to look stunning than not isn't it?'

I was far too happy to let the arsehole dampen my spirits.

'I wish I was coming with you 'he said.

'Shouldn't have made dumb arse arrangements then should you 'I said.

New Year came and went. Mark's heart continued to give him gyp. He started taking a blood thinner causing no end of problems as he had to have it monitored every two weeks to get the dosage correct.

He continued working but not so much on the manual side. I was office admin typing out estimates, invoices and doing the accounts.

In the grand scheme of things we were alright. We had our problems like most couples, but we still laughed a lot and fancied the pants off of each other.

Mark and I turned fifty and forty-five respectively in August 2013. We went all out flying first class to San Francisco where we behaved like proper tourists, visiting Alcatraz, riding trams, taking open top bus tours freezing our tits off despite it being August and stuffing our faces with crab and sourdough bread.

Flew onto to Vegas and partied like ageing rock stars for five nights.

It was a fabulous end to the last summer I would ever spend in ignorant bliss.

PART TWO

Secrets Revealed

Seventeen

Mark had spent the latter part of 2013 converting the loft space in my house into a craft room for me. We were both very tidy people and could not settle if there were chores left to do or the place looked messy. Unfortunately in my case, crafting in any medium left the ground floor of my house looking like a branch of Hobbycraft following an earthquake.

Fed up of crying out in pain every time he stepped barefoot on a rogue bead or finding paint splashes on his favourite Ralph Lauren polo shirt he offered to convert the space if I promised to keep all my crafting paraphernalia up there.

Done deal. I enjoyed having an input and watching it come together. When it was finished I declared it beautiful and to this day it is still my favourite place in the house.

We moved the computer and the business paperwork up there so I could look out over the rooftops as I did my admin work which I openly hated. In actual fact, I pretty much hated anything to do with technology. Bearing in mind at that point I still refused to have a mobile phone. It was one less way that Mark could keep track of me.

There wasn't much need anyway as Mark had the mobile number of nearly every person I knew if he needed to contact me (which he did, on a far too regular basis) and I had my house phone. It amazed me how protective people were about their phones. Near panic attacks if they thought it was lost. Going back home to pick it up if they'd forgotten it as they couldn't bear to be parted for a few hours.

Invariably there would always be a disagreement of some sort when Mark and I worked together. He would dictate estimates that I would type word for word then he'd blame me if it didn't sound right. I'd tell him to write it down instead but his spelling was so appalling I'd spend an age deciphering it.

One morning in early January about half an hour before I left for work Mark called asking if I could send an estimate to one of his customers.

'I'll do it later, if you don't mind. I'm leaving for work soon.'

'Oh please babes, Ray really wants it ASAP.'

It was a rather complicated plumbing job and as I was starting on the second page I asked how much more there was to go.

Eventually we finished with no raised voices for a change.

I was really cutting it fine. We had an audit going on at work and I could not risk being a minute late. I logged onto the emails and one contact in particular caught my eye.

grace67.larson@gmail.com

My initial thought was Larson is a Swedish name. My next thought was do I open it.

A glance at the clock told me I had to leave at that moment to guarantee not being late. With my conscientious mind overriding my curious one I logged off and ran down the stairs picking up my bag shoving my reading glasses and some fruit in it as I left. I got as far as the front seat of my car before a little voice in my head told me to go back and check the email. Retracing my steps running back up the stairs I'd just come down I logged on and waited impatiently.

I opened it to find no words, just an attachment that I opened.

There were three blurry photos.

The first was Mark with a child, a fair haired boy maybe about nine or ten years of age. They appeared to be playing football.

In the second one which was even more blurry than the

first I recognised Paul, Mark's dad standing with another person who was not quite facing the camera.

The third one was a shot of Paul and the unidentified subjects playing what looked like pitch and putt.

I was mystified.

Annoyingly my reading glasses were in my bag which I'd left in the car. The photo's were already out of focus and the more I strained and squinted my eyes to get a better view the worse it got. I began to doubt it was even Mark and Paul at all.

I couldn't waste anymore time. I was in a rush and not concentrating properly. I made my way back to the car and set off for work.

I was mildly suspicious. Just not sure of what. I should have left it and looked again when I got home from work but my impulsive personality wouldn't allow for that. I asked Sue, my colleague if I could borrow her phone as soon as I arrived at work. Unfortunately we were setting up our donation session in a village hall in a semi rural location that had shit service. I wanted to speak to Mark to put my mind at rest. I asked the lovely old girl in the office if I could use her phone. 'Of course you can dearie 'she said but made absolutely no attempt to vacate the room. I called Mark with a slight thudding in my heart. I told myself to stay calm but as soon as I heard his 'Hello 'I lost it.

'Who the fuck is Grace Larson and why are you sending her photos?'

'What photos?'

'Photos attached to an email that you sent to her.'

I could hear the panic in his breathing and sense it in his silence.

'What the fucks going on Mark?'

'It's my son from Sweden, they came over.'

'I'm sorry, I don't understand what you're saying.'

He started to say something just as Sue poked her head in

the office. 'Come on Cleo, team brief is about to start.'

I pressed the button to end the call without saying goodbye.

As I was leaving, the old girl who had been blatantly eavesdropping looked at me over the top of her glasses.

'Trouble at mill?'

'Yeah, I think so 'I answered heavily.

Work that day was interminable. We finished late and I drove home not knowing whether Mark would be there or not. I was tired and all I really wanted to do was shower and climb into bed, which is where I found Mark, lying on top of the duvet watching TV.

'So 'I said by way of greeting.

I stood arms folded across my chest leaning against the door frame not wanting to go near him until I heard what he had to say.

According to him, out of the blue he receives a call from Grace. Hasn't heard from her since his visit years ago. They came over for a few nights at the beginning of January and stayed in a hotel. Mark, Paul and Harry took the boy out while Grace amused herself. He was sorry he didn't tell me but it was just a one off and it wouldn't be happening again.

'You've had all fucking day to come up with something and that's it 'I said incredulously. 'Please, please tell me you are not expecting me to believe that crock of shit. Give me some credit for fucks sake.'

I had left the iPad charging that morning so I went downstairs with a pounding heart and brought it back up to the bedroom. As I logged onto his emails I told him he could point out the people in the pictures as I had my glasses on now and I would be able to see clearly.

Lo and fucking behold, guess what. Deleted. I clicked on trash. Empty.

'I'm telling you, it was me, the old man, Harry and Lucas.'

'And I'm telling you, you're barefaced lying. That wasn't Harry in the photo.'

He insisted it was and with the evidence deleted I had nothing to back me up.

'How old is your son? 'I shot at him.

Shaking his head he said he didn't know exactly. Finally words of truth.

He had told me back in 2002 he was a toddler. Potentially he could be anywhere between thirteen and fifteen.

'Has he got dwarfism?'

Not giving him a chance to react I carried on.

'It's just that the boy I saw in the photo only came up to your waist. Very small for a teenager. Hope he doesn't suffer from little man syndrome when he gets older.'

I asked him if he had anything else to tell me which of course he didn't, just that he was really sorry and would make it up to me.

We went to sleep that night both knowing what each other was thinking. He thought he'd got away with it and I wasn't going to let this go.

His way of making it up to me hadn't changed over the years. Usually extravagant, often unnecessary and on occasion unwanted.

A week later he suggested a holiday. By now I was working thirty hours a week over a three day period. It was really easy to shuffle my roster around to allow me to have a week off work but only use one day of my annual leave.

The email episode had upset me and I wasn't in the mood to go to the pub with him let alone on holiday. In his usual manipulative manner he managed to persuade me to pop into the travel agent next door to the bakers where we had gone to get some fresh rolls on Saturday morning. Before I had time to flick through a brochure he was paying for a holiday to Egypt booking a suite in a fabulous spa hotel. 'You'll love it babes. There's yoga on the beach every morning'.

Of course he was right and I did love it though not just for the yoga. Unexpected sun with warmth and a tan in January was always welcome and we actually had quite a healthy week considering we were on our jollies with unlimited food and drink at our disposal.

On our last night we had a meal in our favourite restaurant and a couple of drinks before heading back early to pack our bags. We made love as we had every night and the animosity I had felt for him a couple of weeks ago had faded to a niggle.

That night I had such a vivid dream that I can still recall it to this day. I was wearing a long white dress that billowed out behind me as I walked barefoot along a corridor that was painted white from floor to ceiling. I walked past several closed doors before coming to one that was slightly ajar. I pushed it open to reveal a large room with a four poster bed. Everything was white and so bright I had to shield my eyes. My mum lay on the bed beckoning me to her. She looked so peaceful. I had a feeling of tremendous happiness as I lay next to her on the bed cuddling into her. She stroked my hair and whispered 'it's his son'.

I woke with a start. My watch read ten past five. I looked over at Mark sleeping soundly beside me. Usually I would nestle into him and that would send me back to sleep but not on that morning. My dream had unsettled me and brought back the feelings of doubt I had surrounding the email and the visit.

The sun had yet to rise but it didn't stop me making my way quietly out onto the large balcony. I took my iPod and settled myself on one of the sun loungers. I shut my eyes and let the darkness and the music relax me back to sleep.

'Morning Gorgeous.'

I woke from my nap to find the sun shining and Mark standing above me with two cups of coffee he'd made from the machine in our room.

We sat in what I'm sure he thought was a companionable silence. I on the other hand was wondering how to broach the subject of the unidentified individuals in the email photos.

The sound of a child wailing came from the path below our balcony. We both looked out to see a man attempting to pacify a toddler and push a double buggy simultaneously. Just as he was explaining it was too early to go in the pool one of the babies in the buggy started bawling and within seconds the other passenger joined in.

'And that's why we should always stay in adults only hotels 'Mark laughed as the noisy little group moved on.

So unwittingly it was Mark who led me very nicely into the conversation I wanted to start.

'Do you ever wish you'd been around more when your kids were growing up?'

It was actually a rhetorical question. We'd had the conversation more than once before and the answer was always the same. No.

I carried on without waiting for a reply.

'Do you think if you had met the right person at the right age you might be happily married with 2.4 children by now?'

'I did meet the right person at the right age, it's just that you didn't feel the same way.'

I groaned at his corniness and told him to shut up, still with a smile on my face.

'Considering you were such a lothario for so many years I'm surprised you've only fathered two children.'

BOOM. And there it was, in the second it took for me to say two children. A blush from under his tanned skin, rapid blinking of his eyelids, a deep swallow and a move towards the sliding doors.

My brain was trying desperately to process what my eyes had just witnessed. I took no satisfaction in seeing and hearing a great thud as in his hurried desperation he walked straight into the glass, bouncing off of it before opening it and entering the room. I followed, slightly unsteady on my legs. My voice, when I spoke was the same as my legs.

'You've got another ch'……I was interrupted before I could finish.

'I can't talk about this here Cleo.'

I went from nought to hysteria in one second flat.

'Oh my god, oh my god, oh my god. 'I began shaking. 'When, oh fuck, how can this be?'

Collapsing on the bed, the towel I had wrapped round myself to sit on the balcony earlier fell from my naked body. I lay there shaking and sobbing while he paced the room like a caged animal.

'Tell me 'I cried. 'Tell me when this happened, how it happened.'

He rubbed his hands over his face as he spoke. 'It was years ago, absolute years ago'.

He came to sit on the bed but I pushed him away with my bare feet. Keep away from me you devious lying bastard.

'I had another son with Lucas's mother, Grace.'

I bolted from the bed just in time to reach the bathroom where I brought up the contents of last night's dinner in the toilet. With my head still hoovering over the pan I asked' How old is he?'

He tried to help me up but I was having none of it.

'How old?'

'I don't know, I really don't know.'

'Six, seven, eight, nine, ten. 'With each number my voice was rising.

'No, older than that 'he said throwing his hands up in frustration.

'We've been together for twelve years Mark. Were we

seeing each other when you fathered this child?'

'NO 'I swear to god, on your life, on Harry's life. We were not together.'

I hauled myself up feeling shaky and weak. I cleaned my teeth and splashed my face with cold water.

'How can I believe you when you won't tell me how old he is. Why won't you put me out of my misery?'

He tried to put his arms around me but I pulled away.

'Please babes, can we just get today out of the way and we can sort out this mess when we get home.'

No fucking way was he sweet talking me.

I threw on a bikini and a cover up, slid on my flip flops, and picked up the beach bag. We weren't being picked up for the airport till four that afternoon and had paid to keep the room on. Not wanting to spend one minute longer with him than I had to I walked out slamming the door behind me.

I have always found comfort from water. Be it swimming in it, bathing in it, showering in it, paddling in it, drinking it, walking by it or looking at it. I needed it now more than ever.

I walked as far along the shoreline as the hotel path would allow me. There was a wooden jetty, empty at that time of the morning. Walking slowly to the end, I perched there dangling my legs over, focusing only on the sound and smell of the sea in an attempt to calm myself down. I don't know how long I sat there for. It could have been ten minutes, it could have been an hour before I heard footsteps behind me. Turning back I saw the familiar stranger that I had spent the last twelve years of my life with. For a few crazy seconds I contemplated sliding off the edge, dropping into the warm clear water below and just swimming in a straight line to see where I ended up.

On second thoughts, though the water was incredibly inviting, the sea level wasn't that deep and landing on a live coral reef would be no fun for me or the coral.

Alternatively, I thought about pushing Mark off in the hope

that a particularly jagged piece of coral would find its way into his heart (if he had one) and pierce his aorta. But I wasn't feeling lucky that day so I remained in my position steadfastly staring out to the horizon.

'I love and adore you Cleo 'said Mark as he crouched down beside me.

He took my face and gently turned it so I had to look at him. Look at a man who I thought I knew as well as my own image in the mirror. A man who was a keeper of secrets. A man who I would never be able to trust again. A man who I didn't want in my life anymore.

I got up suddenly, desperate to get away from the intensity of his puppy dog eyes pleading for forgiveness. Before I had a chance to get away he enveloped me holding my head to his chest.

'Let me go 'I whispered 'please let me go 'I repeated over and over.

'Never let you go, never let you go, never let you go 'came the reply.

Eighteen

A can of worms had been opened in Egypt and the lid wasn't going back on it. I had questions that needed answers and I would not be fobbed off.

Mark answered the most important one the day after we got back from our holiday. Finding out the age of his other son whose name was Alexander would be a game changer for me.

Convincing myself that he had been conceived during our years together it came as somewhat of a pleasant surprise to find out that he wasn't.

However there was another surprise that was decidedly unpleasant. Whilst Mark and I were falling madly in love, Grace was in her third trimester. Preggers. Up the duff. With child. Bun in the oven. Knocked up. Bat in the cave.

Fuck me I thought when he told me. Could this man stoop any lower?

I asked the simple obvious question 'How could you?'

'I had no choice 'he said. 'I knew for a fact that if I told you she was pregnant you wouldn't have carried on seeing me. I know I don't deserve your honesty but please tell me if I was right.'

It pained me to admit it, but he was right. I would have run a mile and not looked back if he had told me. It was pointless dwelling on the what if's. All we could do was live with the decisions that had been made in the past and concentrate on the ones that would affect our future.

I would like to say I was in two minds about staying in a relationship with Mark. If only it were two. My head felt like it contained a hundred minds, each one with conflicting thoughts. Stay, go, stay, leave, love him, hate him, believe him, disbelieve him. It was exhausting.

The next couple of months were precarious to say the

least. I couldn't decide what to do.

I struggled to eat although my appetite for alcohol remained healthy. Mark on the other hand was slightly happier. His secret was out and he just wanted to forget about it and get on with our lives. I was open with him about how I felt and told him more times than I care to remember that I didn't think I was in love with him anymore. He was adamant that he would 'make me love him again'.

I spent a disproportionate amount of time thinking about Grace.

My instinct was telling me that there was far more to this than a secret son. I also knew that any honest conversation out of Mark or the rest of his family would not be forthcoming.

The obvious place to start was Facebook, the most hated website of redundant private detectives the world over.
I made a list of what I knew so far:

email - grace67.larson@gmail.com
name - Grace Larson
age - born in 1967??
mother to two boys aged eleven and fourteen
lives in Sweden

I started my search one Wednesday night in April secure in the knowledge that Mark was ensconced a few miles away in Putney. I poured myself a large glass of wine to calm the trepidation I was feeling as I typed in her name.

I discovered that Larson is to Sweden as Smith is to Britain. There were more Grace Larsons than you could shake a big fucking stick at.

I had conjured up an image in my head of what I thought she looked like and yes, it was the stereotypical idea a lot of us have of the sensible and beautiful Swedes. She would be over five foot nine although I do remember being quite surprised when I saw Ulrika Johnson in Marlow. Very attractive but quite short. She would have natural long blonde hair, big boobs, blue eyes, tanned skin and a sensational figure.

With that in mind I was able to narrow my search down to profile pictures that resembled a cover shot from Sports Illustrated.

A few times I thought I had struck gold only to find she was married with two daughters or not the correct age or lived in Denmark. No luck that first night.

My investigative hours were limited. I felt uncomfortable searching for Mark's past lover with him sitting two feet away while I tapped away on the computer on the nights he stayed over.

He was overstaying his quota at my place. Most weeks he was there for five nights which I found quite claustrophobic. I had a feeling that he knew what I was up to and it made him nervous. He did not want to let me out of his sight but he knew how determined I was and that if I wanted to get to the bottom of something I would.

Late one evening about two weeks after my search had started I got if not to the bottom then certainly two thirds down.

I had been at work and had screened a blood donor with the same maiden name as Mark's sister-in-law Kerry. A thought struck as I asked her to confirm her details. Kerry would be on Facebook. Surely she would be friends with Grace. Their boys were cousins after all. I hadn't seen her or John for a couple of years following a row between the brothers so hadn't been able to ask for their help.

My arse was making buttons to log on to Facebook when I got home from work. I just knew tonight was the night I was going to find her.

It really was as simple as that. I found Kerry easily, checked her friends and there she was. Grace Larson looking absolutely nothing like I'd imagined. More Eastern European than Northern. No blonde tresses hanging down her back, instead, mid brown hair scrapped back from a naturally pretty face, an average size bust and a figure that I couldn't comment on due to the angle of the photo. I hesitated before clicking on her page. Once pressed I could never go back and unknow what it might reveal to me.

Next to the computer was a bowl where we chucked our keys and loose change. I picked up a ten pence piece and decided to let the spin of a coin decide my future. Heads I looked, tails I logged off and that would be the end of it.

I spun the coin and let it land on my hand covering it immediately with my other one. I'm not sure if I had a preference on the outcome.

I lifted my hand to reveal the Queen in profile and I knew what I had to do.

I wasn't that familiar with Facebook but I'd heard people talking about accounts being 'private'. If that was the case I would have to call it a night and reassess my strategy tomorrow.

As luck (or bad luck) would have it, it wasn't and I was in.

The first post was from 2008, written in English, stating that she had grown up a lot in the last few years and how she loved her family both in Sweden and London. Surely she wasn't referring to the Palmers.

I was really only looking for photographic evidence containing Mark so scrolled through quickly noting some posts were in Swedish while others were in English.

There were photos of two boys obviously Lucas and Alexander. I was starting to think I might have been wrong all along when I came to a picture that made me gasp for breath. Mark standing on a patch of grass holding an umbrella flanked on either side by his sons. All three of them. This man just kept stooping lower and lower. Involving Harry in the deception was despicable. By a couple of comments on the photo it appeared they were in Sweden. I carried on searching and by two o'clock in the morning I had all the evidence I needed. There were photos of a trip to the Isle of Wight and even though Mark wasn't in any I had a feeling he was there, standing somewhere out of shot. Another post of a photo, again minus Mark taken at Euro Disney where Grace appeared to be wearing Crocs. This detail managed to elicit a small smile from my otherwise miserable face. Mark and I had a dislike for Crocs that verged on hatred. In all my years in the medical profession I had never even tried a pair on.

It was pointless to even contemplate going to bed with my mind churning over the new information it had just received. I waited until five thirty that morning before I called Mark's mobile. There was no trace of sleep in his hello.

I said in a calm voice' You need to get here straight away'.

There were no questions from him. He didn't ask if I was alright or what was wrong. Nothing but a softly spoken 'Okay'.

He knew. I'm sure he knew that he'd been found out.

Within thirty minutes his key was turning in the lock. I was waiting on the other side of the door. As soon as our eyes met my suspicions were confirmed. He looked nervous and ever so slightly scared. As usual my plans to keep a cool head and not lose the plot went out the window as they always did during confrontations with Mark. I launched straight in with no regard to the early hour of the morning. I screamed and shouted and wailed like a banshee, hardly making sense to myself. Once he heard the word Facebook though, it became all too clear and he sunk down into the armchair with his head in his hands. Even then he didn't realise to what extent he had been exposed. When I brought up Harry's involvement he looked shocked as if he had only just found out about it himself. The worse reaction was when I mentioned the pictures on Facebook from the Isle of Wight.

'She just turned up on the doorstep unannounced and asked me to go with them.'

'Utter bullshit 'was the only answer I could give to that unbelievable comment.

I asked what else had happened over the years, drawing his attention to the fact that there was no point in keeping anything back from me now. He swore blind that there was nothing going on between him and Grace. There hadn't been since he met me and there was nothing more to tell.

'I swear on yo...'

I interrupted him with a roar.

'DO NOT INSULT ME BY SWEARING ON MY LIFE!'

I had shouted so loudly I felt something pop in my throat.

I told him he had to leave, I couldn't stand the sight of him. He begged for me to let him stay and explain. I told him to leave his keys and fuck off.

'Explanations require honesty and I'm afraid that's not an emotion that you're familiar with 'I said as he walked out.

He left the house but only got as far as his Dodge Ram (the very same one that had transported the fam to the Isle of Wight I imagined). He sat outside the house calling the landline continuously until I unplugged it. Every ten minutes or so he would knock on the door and call through the letterbox. Matters were made even worse by the fact I had work that day and there was no way I could get out of it.

I showered and dressed in my uniform noticing that my trousers were getting loose again. These were the second pair I had ordered since February. I didn't own a set of scales so I wasn't sure what I weighed but it was obvious I was losing weight rapidly and not in a good way. Not only had I lost my appetite, I seemed to have lost the ability to swallow solids. Usually a ridiculously fast eater I had taken ten minutes to chew a prawn at lunchtime the day before. It was easier to skip meals and in the evening have a few glasses of wine that seemed to slide down my throat with no problem.

By the time I left for work he had gone. That didn't mean he would stop trying to contact me. No doubt he would be calling or texting one of my colleagues before the morning was out.

As it turned out it was my colleague Sue who had to contact him to inform him I had fainted on session, knocking my front tooth out as I hit the deck and that he needed to come and get me ASAP. Ironic that I had been looking after donors who had just given a pint of blood making sure they didn't faint.

I would rather have called a cab than get in the truck with him but I had no choice. He made such a fuss when he arrived, playing the caring boyfriend to a tee, showing everyone how wonderful he was. He took me to my dentist who saw me straight away and fitted me with a temporary tooth.

I couldn't go back to work. I asked my manager if I could take some unpaid leave for a few weeks which she agreed to.

I looked and felt a complete mess. I hated wearing the tooth as it was wobbly and I kept thinking I was going to swallow it. I pulled it out and flushed it down the toilet. Every time I spoke the words whistled through the gap in my teeth so I stopped talking unless it was absolutely necessary. I couldn't be bothered to wash my hair and went for two or three days at a time without showering. My once plump cheekbones jutted out sharply and my eyes appeared to have sunk back in their sockets. The more I pushed Mark away and the less I looked after myself the more he cared.

He told me I was beautiful which was yet another lie and that we would get through this and that he loved me with all his heart. He let his mum and dad know what I had found out about Grace and the boys on Facebook.

I wondered what his parents reaction would be on seeing me. Surely highly embarrassed, sincerely apologetic, regretful amongst other things. Bearing in mind I hadn't seen Elaine and Paul since January of that year. Nearly five soul destroying months had passed by and I was a shadow of my former self. Not that they noticed that when we popped over to Putney one afternoon at the end of June. By then I had a nice new tooth and had showered and washed my hair especially for the occasion. Within five minutes of exchanging our 'hello's and how are you's 'Elaine had me cornered in the conservatory where I was subjected to her tales of woe. How ill this Swedish situation had made her. How upsetting it had been and couldn't I tell how much weight she'd lost due to the stress. How I resisted the urge to tell her she could do with a bit more stress I'll never know. As for embarrassment, apologies, regret. Not a bit of it. It was as if I was the one in the wrong for poking my nose where I shouldn't.

The next time I saw them was at a twenty first birthday party we had all been invited to.

I hadn't been going out apart from food shopping or to the pool for a swim so it was the first time I had seen people en masse. I had made an effort with my appearance but the person looking back at me from the mirror was a stranger who I hardly recognised. Obviously the guests at the party agreed as several of them walked past me without saying hello not realising who I was. I could tell that for the other guests it was a fantastic party. Top-notch food, free flowing drinks and great music that had everyone up dancing. Lots of love, laughter and warmth which under normal circumstances I would have been in the middle of, drinking it all in. I loved to party and Mark and I were always the first ones on the dance floor. Not that night. I took full advantage of the champagne and managed to make a mini pancetta fig and goats cheese crostini last the whole night. Mark tried to get me up dancing but I was having none of it. He knew better than to push me in my fragile state of mind. It was so obvious to everyone what a mess I was in that I wasn't surprised to receive a card through the post a few days later from Lisa.

To my dearest friend Cleo Laine,

My heart is breaking as I write these words to you. I know what a private person you are so I won't pry BUT, without you saying a word we can all see you are in trouble.
You, the life and soul of every party, the girl who could light up a funeral parlour, the coolest chick I know and so lovely with it. You were the centre of attention on Saturday but for all the wrong reasons. Very upsetting to see you looking so frail. Always remember I'm here whenever you may need me for whatever you may need me for.

Lots and lots of love and hugs
Your dearest friend
Lisa Marie Presley
xxxxxx

Tears rolled down my face dropping onto the card blurring the ink. It was as if the flood gates had opened and once I started crying I couldn't stop. Mingled in with the sadness were some tears of laughter at our nicknames from years gone by. She insisted she was named after Elvis Presley's daughter but as her mum Patsy had pointed out several times over the years she was born six months before the King's daughter.
But the one word that my eyes kept focusing on was 'frail'. It was very hard for me to accept that was how people saw me. I had always been proud of my strength both mentally and

physically. Now it appeared I was losing it and I couldn't let that happen.

Despite the email with the photos attached and the Facebook revelations and the dramas and reassurances that everything was out in the open my gut instinct was still telling me there was more.

I was going to give Mark one last chance to come clean. If he told me the whole truth at least I would know what I was dealing with. If I had the slightest inkling he was still lying the gloves would be coming off.

Nineteen

I presented Mark with his final opportunity to 'tell all 'at the beginning of August. It was a glorious day, clear blue skies with temperatures set to rise somewhere in the eighties. Mark had been supermarket shopping and returned with enough food to feed the street.

He loved to barbecue and he was good at it so I was happy to sit back on a sun lounger with a cold glass of wine and watch him flip, baste and rotate.

I use the word 'happy 'loosely. I'm not sure I had felt anything but sad since January but it wasn't too bad basking in the sunshine being waited on hand and foot.

I was still fragile in mind and especially in body. Being underweight and struggling to eat really upset Mark as food had always been a big part of our lives. I loved to cook at home but we also spent a lot of our leisure time eating out. He had pointed out more than once that if I knocked the alcohol on the head it might improve my appetite. I pointed out that if I knocked him on the head it might improve my life. I heard the timer go off on the oven in the kitchen. Mark had cooked a whole bag of triple cooked chips and he asked if I would mind getting them while he served up the burgers. I specifically told him I just wanted mine plain with no bun. On my return with the chips two minutes later my stomach heaved at the sight of the plate put in front of me. A double cheese and bacon burger with all the trimmings. The grease from the Monterey Jack mingling in a pool of meat juice under the fat toasted brioche bun. He saw my face. 'Just try it Cleo 'he pleaded. I was pissed off. Control freak that he was, he wanted to dictate what I had on my burger.

'I don't have to try it. I know what it tastes like. By serving that up you've managed to put me off completely now you bloody idiot.'

With his face a grimace he suggested I pour myself another glass of wine.

'Oh, I intend to, don't worry about that 'I answered reaching for the bottle in the ice bucket.

I nearly dropped it in shock when Mark slammed both hands down on the table so hard it caused condiments to topple over and cutlery to rattle.

His voice when he spoke was quiet but determined.

'This 'he paused throwing his arms out 'has got to stop. You're killing yourself and in the process you're going to give me another heart attack.'

I offered up a silent prayer - please God.

'When are you going to get over it? 'he asked reaching out to hold my shaking hands.

'When I know what it is I have to get over 'I answered truthfully.

I disengaged my hands from his and held his face close to mine to ensure he couldn't look away when I asked my question.

'Have you been unfaithful to me?'

The answer was in the tightening of his jaw and the delay in his weak 'Never, I swear 'and the tiny beads of sweat that had broken out on his forehead that had absolutely nothing to do with the hot weather.

So my instinct had been right. Time for the gloves to come off as I had promised myself they would. I called my manager on the Monday morning to tell her I wanted to come back to work. I needed some semblance of normality and routine in my life. I arranged to meet Lisa for a coffee. I had not told a soul about the dramas of the last few months even though it was obvious something was up. She was my oldest, dearest and least judgemental friend and I needed to get things off my chest. Before I had even taken a sip of my extra hot skinny latte, Lisa threw me a curveball.

'I know why you've asked us to meet, you're ill aren't you?

Is it cancer?'

Her eyes were brimming with tears and she was shredding a tissue to bits as she spoke.

She took my speechlessness as a yes and said 'I knew it'.

'No, I'm not ill you silly cow although I am heartsick 'I said pulling an exaggerated sad face.

Over coffee and cake I brought her up to date beginning with that first email and ending with my very strong suspicion that he had been unfaithful to me.

It was a no holds barred account and by the end of it I was emotionally drained.

Lisa had hardly said a word through it all but when I had finished she looked at me in bewilderment and asked why the hell we'd met in a coffee shop and not a pub.

Off loading to Lisa and returning to work helped me feel slightly better. I needed to get my strength up to carry out my next plan of attack.

I had made the bold decision to contact Grace. I hadn't needed to write down the email address when I had seen it for the first time on my computer screen back in January. It was etched on my memory never to be forgotten, like the telephone number from the first house I lived in.

Usually impulsive and quite direct I thought it would come easily to me to reel off a few lines and ping it off to Sweden.

It took me half an hour to settle on the first two words.

Hi Grace
Hey Grace
Hiya Grace
Dear Grace
Hello Grace
Yo Grace
Whassup Grace

How did I introduce myself? Did I steam in with my questions straight away?

As much as I wanted answers I had to consider things from her point of view. I was pretty certain she knew nothing of my existence. An email from me might come as a bit of a shock. The last thing I wanted to do was alienate her by asking intrusive questions. I spent so long deliberating over it that I considered adding Merry Christmas at the end of it.

Eventually on Monday 11/08/14 this is what I sent:

Hi Grace,
I'm not sure if you know who I am - my name is Cleo and I am Mark's girlfriend. I apologise for invading your privacy by contacting you like this but I need some answers and feel that you may be the only person that will be honest with me.
Before I go into too much detail please reply to this and let me know if you are okay with it. I fully understand if you chose not to reply but I am hoping you will.
Once again sorry for the intrusion.
Hope to hear from you soon
Regards
Cleo

Please don't let Mark know I've contacted you - he would not be happy about it.

I sent it in the morning just before I left for work so I wouldn't be sitting in front of the computer all day checking for a reply. I convinced myself there would be a reply waiting for me on my return that evening but after logging in and clicking on my inbox thirty eight times I went to bed disappointed.

The next day I was off work. I occupied myself with housework, food shopping and cooking in-between checking my emails. Mark got home just after five and as soon as I saw him I was reminded of how he looked in the weeks leading up to his heart attack back in 2003. I asked him what was wrong and despite his assurances that he was fine the fact that he left his dinner virtually untouched told me he was lying.

Later on that evening when he couldn't even concentrate on the football match on the TV I asked again if anything was bothering him.

'I'm so stressed, I don't think I can cope.'

I was not expecting that answer.

'What are you stressing about? 'I asked concern in my voice.

'I just cant cope 'he repeated.

I went over to where he was sitting in the armchair and crouched down so we were eye to eye.

'You've got nothing to be stressed about 'I said. 'You're probably just tired.'

'Probably 'he said wearily, unable to meet my eye.

The next morning I practically shooed Mark off to work. I was desperate to check my emails for a reply from Grace. I didn't want Mark to be around when I read it. I logged on and there it was.

From Grace
13 Aug 2014 at 09.17

Hi Cleo.
I didn't see your email until yesterday.
I didn't know about you and got in a bit of a shock and I didn't see the last bit of your mail (it was outside the phone frame) so

I have contacted Mark.
If you have questions I will try to answer them as honestly as I can (but remember that it will be my point of view - Mark, if I know him right, will probably have another story).
First answer a couple of mine:

- When did you and Mark start dating?
- How long have you considered yourself to be his girlfriend?
- How did you get this email-address?
It will be interesting to hear from you.
Grace

The first thing that struck me was the sentence - *(it was outside the phone frame) so I have contacted Mark.*

So that was the reason for his stress last night, and there I was giving him sympathy, the bastard. For sure I had questions and her acknowledgment of the fact that Mark may have a different point of view led me to believe that she knew him as well as I did. I began to have serious doubts about anything that Mark had told me. Was Alexander really conceived prior to us meeting. I had taken him at his word when he assured me he was.

Note to self - Never take the word of a pathological liar.

I felt like I had been given an opportunity to finally get to the truth and I was grabbing it with both hands. I read and reread the email until I knew it off by heart. From the tone of it I didn't feel there was much anger, more a feeling of resignation. She was asking me three questions but I knew before I even started typing my reply that I was going to give her a lot more than just three answers.

From Cleo

13 aug. 2014 23:21

Hi Grace,
Thanks for getting back to me.
In answer to your questions:

Mark and I started dating in February 2002.
We split up for approx 3 weeks in January 2008 when he came to see you in Sweden (that was not the reason we split up). He told me he stayed in a boarding house near to where you live but knowing what I do now I don't think that's true!!
When I met Mark he told me he had a young son in Sweden but he did not have very much contact.
I accepted this as his past was nothing to do with me. He never mentioned you or your son - the only thing I ever saw was a photo of your son at his Mum and Dads house.
When he came back from Sweden in Jan 2008 I asked him why he was so secretive about the situation and I said it would be nice if we went to Sweden for a few days and I could meet his son. He agreed and said we would. Months past by and there was still no mention of any contact. Every time I asked if you had been in touch he would become evasive and I began to think he was lying.
We carried on with our lives together - he lives with me and stays at Elaine and Paul's once a week.
I do the administration work for Mark's building company and in January this year as I was going through the emails I saw one had been sent to you (that's how I got your email address) It was photos of Mark, Harry, Paul and your son. I got such a shock as I knew nothing about this visit. Mark said you had been over once to London.
A week or so after seeing the photos we went on holiday to Egypt. On the last day of the holiday we were talking about life in general and I asked him if he thought he may have any other children that he might not know about. I could tell from his reaction that he was hiding something. He said he didn't want to talk about it - I would not let it go and kept pressing him. Imagine my shock when he told me he did have another son

with you. He said he could not remember how old he was. He said he did not see him until he was 16 months old.
I knew he was lying about so much so I found you on facebook (you were a friend of Kerry's, Mark's sister-in-law).
I saw from the photos that there was a lot of contact. Even though there were no photos of Mark I guessed that you were together in the Isle of Wight. When I questioned him about this he told me you arrived at Elaine and Paul's house one day without warning and asked him to go to the Isle of Wight with you.
My questions to you are very personal but I need to know the truth.
Did you get pregnant after I started dating Mark?
Have you stayed in a hotel with him when you have visited London?
Did you share a room in the Isle of Wight?
Have there been any other holidays?
Do you email/text/ring him on a regular basis?
Grace, you are right about Mark - he will have a different story but I cannot believe a word he says.

Look forward to hearing from you,
Cleo

As soon as my finger had hit the send button I was contemplating Grace's reply. There was a teeny tiny hopeful deluded part of me that imagined a reply that read something along the lines of -

Hi Cleo,

Mark and I split up years ago, a few months before Alexander was born. We have an amicable relationship which works well for everybody as it allows us to visit London enabling the boys to spend time not only with their dad but also with other family members. When he visits Sweden he stays at our house but not in my bed of course!! We are in regular contact regarding the boys. I had a feeling Mark was in love with someone else and I'm very happy for you both. Hope to meet you one day.

Bye for now

Grace x

What a foolish and naive woman I was...........

Twenty

From Grace
14 aug. 2014 07:55

Hi again. Forgive me, I have to melt this since it's worse than I thought.
I'll try to answer all your questions later today when I have cooled off and can think straight, but here is info about our sons:
Lucas, born -99, and Alexander born April 2002. Mark came to us when Alexander was 6 weeks (according to him he was in jail after a fight when he was born and waiting for court - that's why it took so long). According to them their mum and dad are together - loving each other but living apart. I thought so too, even if our physical intimacy faded out a couple of years ago, but I thought that was due to his heart medicine.
I'll try and write the rest of the answers later today.

Grace

Her reply released very mixed emotions in me. Knowing for absolute definite that Alexander was born in April 2002 was somewhat of a relief. I did a quick calculation in my head. If Mark saw his son when he was six weeks old that would have been the week in May 2002 that I spent at Patsy and Ron's. Knowing that Mark was telling fanciful lies about being locked up made me laugh incredulously. I felt slightly nauseous at the mention of loving each other but living apart. And finally utterly gobsmacked that Mark would be able to refrain from getting his leg over at every chance he got.

God knows how I managed it but during that exchange of

emails with Grace over those first few days I did not mention anything to Mark. I didn't want to hit him with dribs and drabs of accusations. I needed as much information as I could gather before I delivered the sucker punch. I had to wait until she sent the next email before I confronted him.

Her reply when it came was nothing like I could ever have imagined. Ever. In my wildest dreams or in my worst nightmares.

I had been at work that day, totally preoccupied with the thought of Grace's email waiting for me on my return. I made silly mistakes and was unusually rude to my colleagues. Mark was waiting up for me when I arrived home which was sod's law. I was later than usual and any other time he would be in bed. I wanted to pour myself a glass of wine and get settled in preparation for my nighttime story. Rather than booting up the computer I picked up my kindle from the kitchen worktop. Mark was in the living room and though the downstairs of my house was open plan I stood where he couldn't see me. As soon as I saw the reply was there in my inbox my heart began pounding and my mouth went dry. Mark called out asking me what I was doing. How I wished he would go to bed so I could be left in peace. I told him I was putting the kettle on to make a cup of tea. He insisted on getting up and making it. Once the tea was made he took his back to the living area with a packet of dark chocolate digestives that I knew would keep him quiet for a few minutes at least.

I could wait no longer. I thought I was opening an email.

It turned out I was opening Pandoras box.

From Grace
14 aug. 2014 14:55

Cleo - this is a nightmare. I don't know if I should laugh or cry. Still in shock probably.
Harry wasn't in the pictures you saw: it was of our sons Lucas (15) and Alexander (12) from our trip to London this January.

Answers to your questions:
1. Did you get pregnant after I started dating Mark?
No, but it feels terrible that I was 7 months pregnant with our second child and still under the impression that we might move together sometime - and he was out dating.
2. Have you stayed in a hotel with him when you have visited London?
We have stayed at Elaine & Pauls everytime. Me & Mark in his bed in his room on the top floor, or one of the boys in his bed and I in one of the other bedrooms with our other son as they grew older. Since the fall 2002(?) we have been over to London 2-4 times a year (depending on how many times Mark have been over to Stockholm), 3-6 nights every time.
3. Did you share a room in the Isle of Wight?
Yes - room and bed. Every trip to IoW.
4. Have there been any other holidays?
Yes. Three trips to Isle of Wight:
Last summer (-13) together with Mark, the boys, Elaine &Paul.
The summer before that (-12 or was it 2 years before, -11??? My brain isn't working right now) with only me, Mark &the boys.
And one trip there with Mark, Harry & the boys in the fall a couple of years before that.
We also have been at EuroDisney one fall (2010? 2011?): me, Mark, Harry &the boys.
Elaine & Paul got a photobook of all the trips (except from last summer) where all the years are correct. That includes a picture from Mark & Harry's trip to Stockholm in Aug?/Sept? 2012. Mark & I shared my bed then.
5. Do you email/text/ring him on a regular basis?

Yes. The first years, and when both kids were small, several times a day. Then a couple of years with at least once a day, and now as the boys english are fluent we speak or text a couple of times a week (sometimes less) and Mark calls the boys directly.

More info (if you want it):

Mark has been here several times, mostly for long weekends. 1-2 times a year when the kids were smaller, but after his heartfailure 2003? (if that really happened of course...) it's been more seldom. He stayed in my house, in my bed.
I've never 'just showed up' in London. I've told him well in advance when I'm planning to come over with the boys, and he has participated in the planning of our holiday trips. Sometimes I have booked them and sometimes he has booked them.
June 2007 (when I turned 40) he was here for almost a month, then he went back to London and came back a few weeks after with the intention of moving here. He got cold feet after a week and went back to London. Then he came back in January 2008, again with the intention of moving here but went back to London after 3 weeks. As I recall it he rented a flat in London round the years of 2007-2008, we stayed in it once when we were over during that period.
I'm sorry if the dates and years are wrong. We are staying at our little summer cottage right now, due to renovation of our kitchen, so I can't go back to check my calendars and photo albums. And as I said: still in shock.
Our sexlife has been on hold since I turned 40, I can count the times we've had sex on the fingers of one hand (sorry for being direct), but I thought his impotence was due to his heart medicine. Probably caused by severe guilt I realise now. We have always been cuddly and kissing in bed though. Been less

of that the last couple of years.

Late in June this year he had an unproportionally big outburst about Facebook and me publishing a picture of him - I now understand why.
I'm sorry for this. I've been focused on my shock and pain but I realise that this can't be easy for you either. I hope you have someone you can talk to about this. Since my & Mark's relationship has slowly faded you don't have to worry of any competition from me if you want to try to repair your relationship with him. But I don't want him to disappear out of the boys life and I will do my best to keep this civilized so the boys don't get hurt.
I do have more questions if you can answer them:
- Do you and Mark have kids together? (Need to know)
- When did he move in with you? (Want to know to try to understand and lay the puzzle)

Since I know that I will never get any answers from Mark I hope you and I can keep contact. I know the phases of shock and more questions will rise as time passes.
I will probably have to go to London with the boys when things have calmed down a bit, to establish some form of communication with him so that the boys don't lose contact with him or their grandparents. Maybe in the fall (or even further on - I don't know how long this will take). You and I might even meet up for a drink - anything that will be needed to get closure on this. At least it would piss Mark off....

Grace

My eyes flew across the screen, reading the words just not quite able to take them in. Over to London, sharing beds, holidays, moving in together, Facebook, staying at his flat, sex life, impotence.

My hands had been shaking since reading the first word and by the end of it my legs had joined in. I wanted to see Mark's face when I confronted him with the new evidence but my body had other ideas. I had gone into shock and could not put one foot in front of the other. I felt vomit rise in my throat and as I turned to hang my face over the sink just in case, Mark came into the kitchen area.

'You alright babes? 'He asked full of concern.

I nodded to the Kindle.

'I've had an email from Grace and now I finally know everything.'

I had attempted to scream those words at him but the shock was having a huge effect on me and I could just about whisper them.

His face sagged for a moment but then the adrenalin kicked in flooding his bloodstream sharpening his mental focus to allow him to plan his escape. He bolted for the stairs taking the steps two at a time. As he banged and crashed around in the bedroom gathering his belongings I staggered on jelly like legs to wait at the bottom of the staircase. There was only one way out and I wasn't letting him go that easily. His face when it appeared at the top of the stairs was like a rabbit caught in the headlights.

'I can't cope with this, I can't cope with this 'he repeated over and over as he tried to squeeze past me heading for the front door.

I blocked his way, shoving my face so close to his our noses were touching. 'How could you do this to me?'

He left without answering, leaving me traumatised and desperate for a drink.

I poured myself a brandy as it seemed appropriate following a shock.

I poured myself another as the shock had been so massive.

I poured myself another because it was ever so slightly blurring the edges of my pain.

I poured myself another because I wanted to get shit-faced.

Then I called Mark on his mobile and told him if he didn't come clean with me I was going to kill myself. (He didn't have the monopoly on manipulation). We talked for a long time but the words that actually had any real meaning could have been spoken in under five minutes. He admitted everything Grace had written apart from being unfaithful.

'Funny that 'I said, my slightly slurred speech dripping with sarcasm. 'The one thing I would expect of you and it's the one thing that Grace has lied about.'

We ended the call with him declaring his undying love and me reassuring him I would not take my own life. Like I ever was.

I opened a bottle of wine and sent an email to Grace. It was important to me that she was kept in the loop.

From Cleo
15 aug. 2014 01:50

Grace, you are right, this is a nightmare. I have decided to cry!!!
I cannot believe what I have just read. Thanks for your honesty. I will email you tomorrow as I need time to take this all in. Have just opened a bottle of wine to see me through probably one of the worst nights of my life.
I'm so sorry for the both of us
Will be in contact tomorrow

Cleo.

And it really was one of the worst nights of my life. Comparable only to the night after I found out my mum had four months to live. It was the same unexpectedness of it. I had accompanied my mum to her oncology appointment at the hospital. Her consultant was a warm empathetic woman who had been realistic yet cautiously hopeful when treating my mum's cancer. Following up on scans taken a week before, she wanted to discuss the results. As soon as my mum heard the word deterioration she put her hand up in a gesture that indicated stop talking. She apologised for being rude but said she wanted to leave the room and asked could I help her as she was quite unsteady on her feet by that stage. She held my arm as we walked along the corridor to the hospital coffee shop where I left her sitting with a doughnut and a glass of water. I went back to the room I had just left and knocked on the door. The consultant asked me to take a seat. There was no point in beating about the bush.

'How long has she got? 'I asked.

'I'm doubtful she'll see September.'

My eyes were drawn to the old fashioned calendar blocks on her desk. They read 27/05/00.

So even though I had some experience with shocking news it didn't make it any easier to accept.

I passed out on the sofa sometime in the early hours waking up to a splitting headache and a parched mouth around seven o'clock the next morning. Mark had already left three messages on the answerphone but I was in no mood to speak to him. I was glad of my hangover. It dulled my senses, tired me out and enabled me to drift off to sleep for short intervals at least. I had to get my head together to type Grace a reply. She was the only person I wanted to be in contact with.

Twenty-one

From Cleo
15 aug. 2014 21:21

Hi Grace,

With a heavy heart and an aching head I type this email. The wine I drank last night did not help me sleep. I had to re-read your email several times before the facts sunk in and I've spent all night going over and over it's contents.
Let me tell you what has happened - After reading your email I confronted Mark late last night and in true Mark style he began to deny everything - he ran upstairs and started packing a bag. He was like a rabbit caught in the headlights. He left the house and drove off. I called him on his mobile and we talked for a long time. He admitted everything you said apart from being unfaithful - he said he had not slept with you since Alexander was born. (He knows how strongly I feel about being faithful).
Grace, I would love to say I believe Mark but I know in my heart that you are telling me the truth.
(at least I hope you are).
Okay, a little background information:
Mark got married to his second wife in 1997 (I think it was April though I cannot be sure of the month). I'm sorry if this is another shock for you as I know Mark did not tell you he was married when you got together.
Cathy was his first wife (they got married when Mark was about 25) - Harry's Mother
As I already told you I met Mark in Feb 2002 at which point he was still married. Within a day of meeting each other he had

left his wife. Mark moved out of his marital home and back in with his parents. I continued to live in my flat in Chelsea before later moving into the house I'm in now.
Can you believe at one one point in his life Mark had a wife, a pregnant girlfriend and a new girlfriend all at the same time?
If I remember correctly Mark was in Spain with me when he told you he was in prison. He denies he said this and says he did not see his son when he was 6 weeks old - again who do you think I believe!!
Of course you must have seen the tattoo on his arm - that's my name in Chinese writing. He had that done a couple of months after we got together. I would be interested to hear how he explained that.
In answer your questions:
Kids together:
No, we do not have children together - Thank god!
When he moved in:
Mark has been staying here most nights for about 5 years - no wonder he always had to keep a room at his Mum and Dad's - I suppose he told you he lived there.
I am still trying to understand how his Mum and Dad have been able to face the both of us.
Mark and I went to the IoW in October 2012 with Elaine and Paul to celebrate their 50th wedding anniversary. How could they have done that knowing their son was cheating on 2 women - we were all together at a family party in July of this year.

I am still so raw I cannot even get my thoughts in order.
I have close friends who I can talk to but what's the point, they have no idea what this feels like.
I have one friend who would chop Mark's balls off if I told her the full story!!
Grace, this has been so painful for us both but in a strange way it has been a comfort to know that I am not alone - we have

both been taken for fools!!
Who knows what's going to happen now. We must keep in contact and we will meet up for a drink or 2 when you come over. I have an idea: You me and Mark go for a drink in Putney - we get him drunk and throw him off Putney bridge, at least that way he would no longer be a menace to women!!!
Get back to me with your thoughts

Cleo

From Grace
16 aug. 2014 00:17

My thoughts? Let's meet up for a drink with Mark, Elaine AND Paul and throw them ALL in the river.
This is just crazy - I've gone hysterical after reading your email. I can't stop laughing. The image of rabbit-Mark is so spot on and the info about Mark being married a second time and being married DURING our first years is just too much. Thank you for confronting him - I hope he suffers deeply. I don't think I'll ever get the chance since he probably will avoid me.
Of course we have had sex after Alexander was born. How can he even think that its worth to continue the lying?? Or is he living so strong in denial that his memory gone blank? But as I said: our sexlife has faded over the years. But the cuddles, kisses and "I love you's" have been there.

I sent an email to Elaine yesterday and told her that I knew about Mark's charade (since I understood by your mail that they must be aware of Marks double-life). I don't want them to lose contact with the boys and I wanted them to know that the blame is Marks. Imagine my surprise today when I got Elaine's reply: she was so sorry I found out about this. "We live after the old saying - 'what you don't know wont hurt you' " Not a word about that they think their son has done something wrong. They were more interested in knowing who told me. I didn't tell them that you contacted me. I now think that they all must be psykopats in that family. How the hell can they think that this is ok as long as no one knows???? And everytime when we've been over - all the pictures of the boys in the living room, and of me and the boys in Mark's room - have they all been a part of 'setting the scene' for our arrival???

Since I love to take photos I have loads of proofs of Marks visits here and of us in London. If your ever in doubt I mean. Beautiful pictures of a 6-week-old Alexander in the sunshine in his fathers strong tattoed arms... Very painful to think about that now. The tattoo? "It's all my boys names in Chinese"... I was very happy about it. Now I wish I knew Chinese at that time....

I think he's blamed prison a couple of times. One New Years when I was pregnant and hysterical and couldn't reach him to say 'Happy New Years' and when it comes to Alexander birth it might have been that he blamed he was waiting for a court date. I might be mixing up his excuses for not showing up since they have been so many: prison, court dates, not finding passport, missing flights, loads of work, burglary in the flat, Harry needs to be sorted out, fear of flying etc etc...

Feels like you are my only lifeline to answers - THANK YOU for being brave enough to contact me! I still haven't spoken to Mark. Feels like I have nothing to say, and that there is nothing I want to hear from him. Must get in contact some day though and let him know that I wont stand in the way for his relationship with the boys. They love, adore and need him.

Keep in touch!!

Grace
(Margaritas is my painkiller for the night)

I decided I was going to have to get some beta blockers and take two before I read anymore emails from Grace in the future. I was in serious danger of having a heart attack though the thought of Mark finding me dead, slumped over the keyboard with Grace's email on the screen did have a touch of poetic justice about it.

I had taken no pleasure in informing her of Mark's marital status when they first got together. Grace had more than her own feelings to consider. Both her sons were conceived and born while their dad was married to another woman. They were still young. In fact it couldn't possibly have come out at a worse time for them. Lucas at fifteen was bang in the middle of his teenage years. With his puberty hormones on the increase, it was bad enough that he had to deal with oily skin, spots, peer pressure and girl trouble. Finding out that his errant father had been cheating on his loyal (I think) mother could cause a certain amount of psychological damage. Alexander was twelve. He still had the pleasure of wet dreams and his first body hair to come, with no dad around to talk about it with. They were too old for the truth to be kept from them. I had no qualms about Grace handling the situation with sensitivity, it was Mark I was worried about. His son's may have loved adored and needed him but I wasn't so sure the feeling was mutual.

I wasn't overly bothered at the mention of the kissing and cuddling. I was still reeling from the shock that their sex life was sex dead. I was getting more than my fair share with him so it was only just that she got a few kisses and cuddles now and again. Apparently Mark had told his second wife he loved her the night before he left her so I wasn't putting too much stock into the feeling behind his use of those words. Having said that I didn't doubt for a minute that he had loved Grace at one time. He probably did still love her but in a different way. I hadn't had that conversation with him yet and I could not begin to predict which way he would play it.

Thinking about Mark's mum and dad and the significant part they had played in the charade made my already simmering blood boil. I had seen one photo of Lucas in the hallway in all the years I had been visiting that house and whenever I was in Marks bedroom it was a photo of me beside his bed. When I read the sentence 'I now think that they all must be psykopats in that family 'I nearly fell off my chair laughing. I think it was the Swedish spelling that done it. The word looked much harsher with a 'k 'and somehow more sinister. She could not have given a more simple yet accurate description.

And how I wished too that Grace had spoken Chinese. All his boy's names indeed. His imagination knew no bounds especially when it came to excuses. When I read about those I could not find one iota of truth in any of them: prison, court dates, not finding passport, missing flights, loads of work, burglary in the flat, Harry needs to be sorted out, fear of flying etc etc...

Granted, he had been in a young offenders detention centre but he was eighteen at the time. There had been court dates but again many years ago before Grace and I came along. He knew the whereabouts of his passport at all times. It was usually in a drawer at my house. He would be the last person to miss a flight, partly due to the fact he loved flying. The further the better as far as he was concerned. Every time we had been on holiday regardless of the destination he liked to get to the airport about three hours before take off to do a bit of shopping and have a few drinks. The flat which he had actually lived in for nearly three years had remained safe, secure and free of unwanted visitors.

And if Harry ever needed sorting out......Mark would be the last person to do the sorting.

From Cleo
16 aug. 2014 10:13

Grace,
Another sleepless night spent going over and over this mess trying to make some sense of it all. Mark did not stay here last night - he said he was going to stay at his mum and dad's. He is coming home later this morning and I will be waiting for him with a long list of questions that I want answers to. I will lock the door and hide the key so he cannot run away like he always does.
I know him well and he will be desperate at this point as he can see his life falling apart. It will be interesting to hear what lies he will come out with today. He cannot stand being questioned probably because he cannot give truthful answers. He is a pathological liar and always has been.
Should we be surprised at the way Mark has turned out bearing in mind he has been brought up by 2 parents who clearly think it is acceptable to cheat and lie your way through life.
Grace, if it makes you feel any better I have had the "what you don't know won't hurt you" line from Elaine as well. She said it to me once when I asked her something about Mark. I should have realised then what they were all capable of.

Where do we go from here?
Are you going to tell your sons that you and Mark are not together?

Like you say, it is important that they remain in contact with their Dad however much of an arsehole he is!! They should not be affected by all of this shit that's going on.
Anyway would you want your sons brought up with Mark's morals - look at what he has already taught Harry - yes Harry it is totally acceptable to have affairs and lead a double life. It upsets me so much to think that Mark has had to tell Harry to lie to me.
As for the pictures in the house and in Mark's room. No wonder we never visited Elaine and Paul unannounced. Mark always rang to say we were going over - once we were passing and I suggested popping in for a coffee. Mark pulled the car over and rang his mum to tell her we were coming (we were 1 minute away from the house) I wondered at the time why he would do that - now I know, so Mr and Mrs honesty could rearrange their pictures!!
I don't know about you but as the shock of all this is wearing off very slightly I am beginning to get angry and I mean SERIOUSLY angry.
Do you want me to let you know what happens today?
Come on Grace, admit it, you cannot wait to hear what bullshit is going to pour out of Mark's mouth now.
Do you think it can get any worse, is there more to come? Was he leading a treble life?!!
Try to have a good day - I'm going swimming now to try and lose some of this anger.

Cleo

I went for my swim and returned home to find Mark waiting for me. I was slightly taken aback at how dreadful he looked, seeming to have aged ten years overnight. Not that I was offering any sympathy. Although determined to get answers to my questions I knew it was not going to be easy bearing in mind I was dealing with a man who told lies for fun. I was going to have to use my savvy. I eased him fairly gently into what he thought was a conversation but in actual fact was along the lines of an interrogation. I put on my best Jane Tennison impersonation and got to work.

I confused him with my first question.

'So are we still going on holiday to Turkey?'

We had booked it in advance the year before to celebrate our birthdays at the end of August.

'Of course we are 'he said.

'It'll be lovely won't it 'I said, a dreamy soft tone to my voice.

He breathed a sigh of relief, happy the conversation was going much better than he expected.

I continued in the same tone. 'Alternatively, I could go to Turkey and you could go and spend time with your not so secret family in Sweden.'

I watched as his face reddened as he looked away from my stare. 'They're not my family 'he mumbled.

'Well, someone had better tell them that.'

It was taking every ounce of my self control to keep a lid on the anger that was bubbling through my veins. I felt it seeping out of my pores poisoning the air between us.

'Why did you continue to lie to me after I found out about Alexander? Why didn't you use it as an opportunity to come clean?'

He shook his head as he spoke. 'I just couldn't face it. There hadn't been anything going on with Grace for so long I convinced myself there was nothing to tell you.'

At this point the lid came off and my anger was released. 'Sharing a bed, kissing and cuddling and exchanging 'I fucking love you's 'and you think there's nothing to tell me?'

I brought that part up first as I knew he would be horrified that I was aware of such intimate details. If I was a betting girl I would have laid money on his next sentence, a lot of money.

'I didn't love her 'he said.

'I never asked you if you did but as you've made that statement I think you should elaborate.'

By now I was up on my feet standing over him with my hands on my hips.

'You can't hurt me anymore. I'm done. You've broken my heart and you damaged it in the cruelest way possible, not in one go but over a sustained period of time. The very least you owe me is a bit of honesty. Don't open your mouth to me unless the words are true.'

'I did have feelings for her but it was nothing like what I feel for you. Don't you think if she was that important to me I would have left Sarah (his second wife) for her. Don't you think I'd have stopped playing the field. Christ Cleo, I was sleeping with a different girl practically every month up until I met you.'

'How bloody decent of you to cut it down to just me and Grace 'I pointed out.

'I even had a fling once with another Swedish woman who I met on the flight back to London from Sweden 'he said looking sheepish.

'Seriously Mark, do you actually have a conscience?'

'I wasn't unfaithful to you 'he insisted.

'Bollocks 'was the only comment that lie deserved.

Mark admitting that he had slept with another woman was neither here nor there. I know most people who find out that their partners have cheated drive themselves half demented with torturous visions of their loved one with another making mad passionate love. I was quite unlike most people. Mark had slept with so many women that the thought of him slipping his dick inside one had lost its intimacy and importance for me. My mum always told me to pick my battles. This particular one could wait for another day.

I moved on to question him about the role his parents had

played over the years.

'Did you threaten your parents with a slow painful death if they told me about Grace and her TWO sons or were they quite happy to go along with it so they could play happy families?'

'My mum kept on at me to tell you.'

'Was that before or after your trip to the Isle of Wight? You know the one I mean, when Grace and the boys turned up on the doorstep in Putney asking you to accompany them on a spontaneous galavant. What luck that you were all indoors with nothing planned and were able to pack your bags. AND to get booked onto the ferry from Southampton which can be quite tricky if not booked in advance. We know that from our trips there don't we?'

I was mocking him and it gave me some satisfaction to see that he was clearly mortified.

'I did it for my mum and dad he whined.'

I completely ignored him and carried on talking.

'Of course it wasn't just your mum and dad with starring roles. Harry had a big part too. Taking him to Sweden and the Isle of Wight and not forgetting Euro Disney which was obviously the boys only holiday that you lied about so easily.'

'Please don't blame Harry for anything. 'Mark pleaded. 'He was only doing what I told him to do.'

'Did the same apply to your brother and his wife? 'I shouted back. 'Were they just doing what they were told?'

'Cleo, you're making out like there was loads of involvement. They came over here about twice a year and only ever for a few nights. I tried to arrange it to coincide with you being away but sometimes it didn't work out like that. It was nerve racking for me with them staying in Putney thinking you might pop over.'

'Nerve wracking for you 'I repeated. 'Oh you poor thing, please forgive me if I don't get my violin out.'

I continued to bombard him, alternating between

revelations from Grace's emails and pursuing my line of pertinent questioning. We talked, or rather Mark talked while I shouted, swore and screamed at him till the early evening. By then I'd had enough for one day but warned him that we would continue tomorrow as there were still things I wanted to know. He agreed and assured me he would do whatever it took to keep us together.

Twenty-two

After ordering a take away and knocking back a few glasses of a heavy red wine each we slept surprisingly well considering the turmoil we were in. We fell into our natural positions in bed with Mark spooning me as usual. I did not even consider sleeping in the other bedroom. Feeling his skin on mine, his breath on my neck, his strong arm pulling me into him was the calmest I had felt all day.

The next morning lying in bed sipping the cup of tea Mark had made me I checked my emails and saw there was one from Grace. For a moment I imagined how she must feel hundreds of miles away, not knowing what was going on. I had to hand it to her. She was more composed than I would have been in her situation. After reading that first email from me I would have been on the next plane out of Sweden.

And I most definitely would have just turned up on the doorstep unannounced, preferably armed with a sawn off shot gun.

From Grace
16 aug. 2014 14:53

Cleo, as it sinks in more and more that it's been ME who has been 'the other woman' - not once, but twice as it's showed - I'm getting more and more numb. Can't even get angry with him - just think he is pathetic. I'm happy you are angry enough to not let him get out of this easy!! (Do get unproportionally VERY angry with Elaine Paul for some reason).

To get your emails is the only things that keep me sane right now and I'm ready to hear everything you want to tell me. I

don't think you're gonna get the truth or answers from him though. It will be too easy for him to say he never loved me - when I'm not there and he has to look me in the eyes when he says it - and that he only pretended to have a relationship with me so that he could see the boys. Trust me - I have always made it clear to him that of course he would continue to see the boys even if we were not together. That's why I can't figure out why he's continued the charade? Could be that he has always wanted an option open - he seems terrified of getting tied down.
Of course I haven't got any proofs of us sleeping together while seeing you - he will continue denying that I think. I do have a video from us having sex together (but I think we took it before he met you) - but since he seems a bit lost when it comes to dates and years you can try to use the knowledge of it as a way of getting him to admit him cheating - not only emotionally but also physically (he'll be so stressed he won't remember when we filmed it. Come to think of it - he was actually MARRIED then!!!!).
I haven't told the boys yet that we are not together any more and that he now lives with someone else. I don't have any problems in doing that but I don't want to risk that Mark still will be in his disappearing mode so that the boys feel that THEIR relationship has changed and they can't talk to him. I have always told the boys that it's better to tell about unpleasant things straight away since it gets worse if you don't - Lucas lives after that but Alexander is acting a bit more like his father. I'm trying desperately to think of a way to use this situation as an example without them starting to hate their father or (even worse :-) taking after him...

My mind is with you and I'm looking forward to hear from you again.

Grace (with a Margarita headache today...)

I silently thanked Grace for sending me new ammunition. I could tell that it was important to her to get the recognition she deserved for the part she and the boys had played in Marks life. Sadly she had underestimated his ability to cut people out of it at the drop of a hat. I knew if I wanted to manipulate the situation I could get him to promise me he would have nothing more to do with Grace and the boys and he would have been more than happy to agree. He wouldn't actually be doing it to keep a promise to me, he would be doing it because it suited him. He would prefer me to be angry with Grace so we could bitch about her and agree what an awful woman she was, a liar and a fantasist who had deluded herself for years. Sorry Mark, there was no chance of that. How could Grace and I feel anything but sorrow for each other.

By lunchtime I felt he hadn't been put through the wringer enough. I had two more questions to ask him before I was done.

'What did the affair mean to you Mark?'

'I keep telling you it wasn't an affair. It was me seeing my boys, trying to keep things separate so nobody would get hurt. Grace is a lovely woman who has done a great job of bringing those boys up and I take no credit for it. I knew what I was doing was wrong but I just blocked it out of my mind. When I was with you I hardly gave them a thought. Years ago it was easier for me to justify what I was doing. You and me were constantly arguing and fighting, splitting up and getting back together. You made me feel useless, you've never needed me for anything and you made that quite clear when you used to insist I had to leave you alone because you needed a break from me.'

'How bloody convenient that must of been for you. I bet you were straight on the phone to her making arrangements as soon as you left me.'

'Not at all Cleo. I had ample opportunity to get on a plane to Sweden. You won't want to hear this but I was always welcome there. Instead I chose to stay around waiting for your call to say it was okay to come round.'

I did believe that part. I thought back to those times following a row when he would hang around my house or my work for days on end trying to convince me to talk to him.

My second question was 'Why do you want us to stay together?'

'Because I love you, I absolutely adore you. I would chose to be with you rather than anyone on this planet. You're beautiful, you make me laugh, you're crazy and my life would be shit without you.'

From Cleo
19 aug. 2014 01:38

Grace, this is such a hard email to write.
Mark and I have spent the last 3 days going over this mess.
We have talked/screamed/shouted and cried. I am emotionally drained. The outcome is that we are staying together. I know you must think I am crazy but I cannot imagine my life without him in it. He has been with me through so much, both good and bad. I have to face up to the truth, put it behind me and move on. Only time will tell if we have made the right choice.
I don't want to hurt you by telling you things you don't need to know and I cannot take anymore pain. I am so unbelievably sad and sorry about all that has gone on. We must both find strength from somewhere and carry on.
Mark still wants to see his sons in the future and I know you would not stand in the way of that.
I know I am probably going to regret the choice that I have made - after all a leopard never changes its spots.

Only time will tell. You are in my thoughts.
Cleo

From Grace
19 aug. 2014 13:22

Thanks for letting me know Cleo.

I have sent a text to Mark that I'll contact him this week about the economic arrangements concerning the boys. I'm not sure if he had a special phone handling our relationship (and has now thrown it away or keeping it off) so I'm not sure he has got the text. He and I have to sort the terms out by Monday, after that I let the Swedish authorities handle that with him instead.
I'll tell the boys in a couple of weeks - I want them to start school after the summer break and go back to normal routines before telling them. The first time they come over to London after this I'll probably go with them so that they can see that their mum and dad can face each other (I don't want them to start disliking him for hurting me). I'll let you know when so that Mark don't have to lie about it. I'll make him pay for a very VERY luxurious room for me in a nice hotel (without him in it of course...).

I don't think you are crazy. It's a human reaction after such a shock, and after several days of emotional turmoil anyone would want to get back to normal tracks.
Thank you for contacting me so this charade didn't have to go on, and if you further down the line still want to have that drink and throw one (or more people) off the Putney Bridge I'm all up for it!

Grace

I didn't think Putney Bridge was long enough to line up the number of people I wanted to throw off of it. I had declared to Mark during our reconciliation talks that every single adult that was aware of the existence of Grace and myself and kept their mouths shut was a prize cunt. He didn't argue which lead me to believe he probably agreed with that statement.

As far as his mobile phone was concerned, there was only one and it wasn't switched off. It was the same number as the day I met him. I had never so much as glanced in the direction of his phone let alone checked it. I had been without one for so many years that they held no interest for me whatsoever. Mark was not going to be very happy about discussing 'economic arrangements'. In England that translated to maintenance payments. Mark was generous to a fault when it was off his own back. When the choice was taken out of his hands it was a different story. I genuinely hoped that they could sort things out amicably. It was so important where children were involved. At that stage I felt confident it was possible and I looked forward to meeting Grace although I thought it best we avoid arranging to meet anywhere near Putney.

From Cleo
20 aug. 2014 10:43

Hi Grace,

I hope you manage to sort out arrangements amicably. I will do the best I can to make sure Mark faces up to his responsibilities.
He told me once that he was in trouble with the Swedish authorities regarding maintenance for Lucas (at that time I only knew about 1 son) and could possibly have gone to prison. Probably another one of his warped stories.
Do you think he is a frustrated gangster - he seems to tell a lot of lies involving criminal activity!!

Of course we will meet up - how could we not after all we've been through. Stay in a hotel with a good bar and we will go through every drink on the cocktail list. He can pay for that as well. If I start plotting revenge on the Palmer family you must stop me drinking!!

Keep in contact - I know I will be relying on you more to tell me what's going on than Mark......

I am here if you need to talk

Take care,

Cleo

Looking back it is astonishing that a few days after I sent that email to Grace, Mark and I boarded a plane at Gatwick and headed off to Turkey. I don't think either of us had ever been in more need of a complete break. I just wasn't sure if we should have been going on separate ones.

My emotions were like a whore's drawers. Up and down, day and night. The anger was leaving me, to be replaced with a sadness that seemed to weigh me down. We could be at breakfast on the terrace looking out at a cloudless sky meeting a shimmering sea and tears would trickle down my face. Mark would ask me what was wrong but I had no answer. We made love one night and I cried like a baby when it was over. Mark held me and soothed me until I fell asleep in his arms. Then suddenly it would be like the fog clearing and I would be jittery with positive thoughts. My energy levels would soar and Mark would find me in the hotel gym having been on the treadmill for an hour. I would talk incessantly about jack shit and was able to drink copious amounts of alcohol without it having any effect on me. I'd swim too far out to sea, secretly enjoying watching Mark waving manically from the beach, his demands for me to come back, lost in the distance between us. I would release some, but not all of the air from my lungs, raise my arms above my head and glide down under the water, like a free diver sinking towards the sea bed. It was dark and cold and I felt as if I was in a giant womb. I had to stop doing that after Mark screamed for the lifeguard from the pool area to swim out and rescue me. Towards the end of the holiday I calmed down somewhat and realised I had probably been suffering from a rather extended mental breakdown that had started back in January. I had to pull myself together and get on with it.

As bizarre as it sounds, I actually felt better that the whole truth had finally been uncovered. It wasn't as if Mark was in a dilemma over which woman to choose. I felt confident of his love for me. He had always been an 'actions speaks louder than words 'kinda guy and I knew without a shadow of a doubt that if he had wanted to begin a new life in Sweden he would have got on a plane in January if not years before. On the subject of which, he hated the fact that I was encouraging him to go to Sweden to see Grace and the boys, to talk things through and let the boys know that his relationship with them remained the same. I had no qualms about him being with Grace. It sounded like the passion was long gone from their relationship so I wasn't worried about them falling into bed together. Deep down, despite my daily reminders to sort out a flight and get his arse over there I knew he would probably never step foot on Swedish soil ever again.

Twenty-three

From Cleo
19 sep. 2014 20:35

Hi Grace,

It's me again.
You must dread reading an email from me - hopefully the contents of this one will be nicer than previous ones I have sent. I hope all is well with you.

Mark tells me you are thinking of coming over in October. If the Swedish school holidays are the same as England I am assuming that it's the end of October. He said Lucas is anxious about flying but Alexander wants to see him.
Mark has suggested that if you were willing to let Alexander fly over on his own they could stay here together in our house. Obviously I want to meet Alexander (that's if he wants to meet me) but I don't want to overwhelm him. I would imagine he just wants to be with his Dad. I wouldn't stay here as it might be a bit much for a first visit. I could stay with a friend to give them some time together.

Is that right that he called Mark a dickhead when you told him what was going on? If he did I like him before I've met him. You have obviously brought your sons up to be good judges of character!!!
Even if you do come over with one or both boys don't you think it would be good for them to stay here with Mark?
I totally understand if you are uncomfortable with the thought of the boys being introduced to me before I have met you so

just let me know what you think.
Just to let you know the house is a smoke free zone so you won't have to worry about passive smoking like you do in Putney - I feel like I've been kippered when I come out of that house!!

If you do come over of course you are invited here - you must see where the boys will be staying in the future.
I am going to suggest to Mark that we visit Sweden - I have never been and from what I have seen it looks fantastic. We could come for a weekend and stay in a hotel. I would be quite happy wandering around on my own so Mark could spend time with the boys.

Mark doesn't know I have sent this email - I think he is uncomfortable with the fact we are in contact - maybe he thinks we will compare notes!!!

Get back to me with your thoughts.

Cleo

From Grace
23 sep. 2014 23:22

Hi Cleo.

Sorry for the late reply - I've spent the weekend away with my friends (not many Mark-supporters there now...) and then I

went straight to a two-day conference at work.
All your suggestions about London and Sweden visits sounds good. But I think it's too soon.
Both boys need to see their father, but they've said that they want everything to be as normal as it can for them. And if they come to London they need to spend time with their grandparents as well. I want the boys to ask about the new situation and be curious, instead of pushing new things on them.
I said to Mark that I will email you and let you know if I book a flight to London so that he knows that it's no point in keeping things in the dark. I have not booked anything yet though - you can be assured that I will let you know if I come over.
Right now I don't know what we will do though. I will talk to Mark to try to figure out what's best for the boys at this point and then let you know.
Take care!
Grace

The first thought I had after reading the email was the fact that she had obviously told if not all, then at least some of her friends about Mark and his dirty shenanigans. I on the other hand had told no-one apart from Lisa. Had I kept quiet to protect Mark from my friends disdain and contempt? Was my silence the only way I could guarantee that they would not lambaste me for my questionable reactions to Mark's appalling behaviour. Whatever my reasoning behind it I was keeping schtum. I had enough on my plate without having to deal with other people sticking their oar's in. It shouldn't really have been my concern but the most important thing for me at that moment was to make sure that Mark saw his sons and tied up any loose ends with Grace. I was more than surprised that she seemed keen for the boys to stay with their grandparents. I had seen Elaine once since my initial contact with Grace. My heart sank when Mark had suggested popping in to see his parents. In a bid to get back to normal I agreed begrudgingly. I wasn't in the door five minutes before she informed me that she'd received an email from Grace. I knew this already as Grace had told me but decided to play it dumb.

'Oh did you'? I asked looking surprised.

'Don't know who she thinks she is sending me things like that. She typed in great big letters 'I KNOW ALL ABOUT MARK AND CLEO'. I don't know how she managed that.'

It was on the tip of my tongue to say 'Er, it's called caps lock you stupid woman 'but I somehow managed to refrain myself. Instead I asked her how she could sleep at night knowing what she did.

If she had chased me out of the house hitting me with a broom it would have been worth it just to see the 'How dare you ask me that 'expression on her face.

'Come on Elaine, I'd like to know how you sleep soundly in your bed every night?'

May God forgive me but I was enjoying myself.

'Mark told us we could never tell you. I told him to tell you many times but he said you would leave him. He's always said he loved you. Grace was deluded. 'Elaine continued in full flow indicating the kitchen table we were sat around. 'She sat here once and I asked her when she was going to get herself a boyfriend. She said why did she need a boyfriend when she had a big handsome man already.'

At that point the big handsome man in question walked into the kitchen and our conversation was over. Had we not been interrupted I would have pointed out that if Grace was deluded it was only because when she had been in this house she had been surrounded by deluders.

If Grace wanted to turn down my offer of the boys staying at my house in favour of them staying with their grandparents that was fine by me. I could not have been more accommodating. It was time to take a step back and let

Mark and Grace sort it out between them. I wasn't expecting to receive another email so quickly and I was totally unprepared for its contents.

From Grace
24 Oct 2014 at 22.30

Hi Cleo.
Here comes a status update from what's going on here:
The boys need to see their father, and I need to get closure on a 16 year relationship.

1,5 months ago the boys thought their mum and dad loved each other. Now they know they are not together any more and that above this, their dad been involved with someone else the whole time.
Lucas is fine with it he says, as long as it doesn't affect him and that he doesn't have to see you. He wants to be with his dad, and meet Harry, and when he is in London to stay with grandma & grandpa and that his dad is going to be there. This is what he said when he found out and this is how he still feels.
Alexander - who is younger - is very angry. With Mark, and with you. But he loves his dad of course. But he is very affected by the fact that you exist, and he has called you loads of things and he hates you. I have every time this comes up said that Cleo didn't know and it is not her fault, but he still says "I don't even want that girl to come over the Swedish border". It is not easy for him to grasp this.
Mark knows that this is the boys reactions and feelings. He also knows that I need to sit down and talk to him so we can end this relationship in a proper way. I need closure, and after 16 years I think I deserve that, and not just to get the information in an email from his current girlfriend. I have also told him that I will contact you with anything involving him and me

meeting, so he knows I will tell you if I come over to London or if he comes over here.
At this point I think he should come over to Stockholm to show the boys he makes the effort and that he wants to see them. And to make less hassle for me. He needs to give them his undivided attention when he is here, and be here when they go to sleep and when they wake up - as usual. He or I can stay on the couch, or I can stay at my parents or at my friends - depending on how much we are able to talk things through. And I will need to talk to him to be able to move on. At least you have had that possibility.

As I said before - I have no interest in him as a man anymore. Even though I am a very understanding person, and can forgive most things because I know we are not more than human, but a man that can act like this and has behaved the way he has for so long, is not someone to be in a relationship with. And he will keep withholding truths, because he is not able to make decisions and stand up for what he thinks is right if it means someone is getting hurt or angry. That makes him feel unpleasant and for some reason he cant take that. Upbringing? Rejection? Borderline personality? Other damages? Whatever it is I don't care - he doesn't seem to want to work on it or figure it out himself and then it is hopeless. He acts exactly like an alcoholic, with the lies, broken promises, deceiving etc, but instead of drowning unpleasant feelings in alcohol, he drowns them in lies, trying to keep everyone happy so he doesn't have to have anyone have a go at him. The result is totally the opposite though...

If you and Mark still are together a couple of years down the line then of course you will see the boys and be involved in that part of Mark's life (I think that is what you want - I would have wanted that after being kept in the dark for so long). They boys will probably be calmer about this and have grown an interest in meeting you, when they have felt that you haven't been in the way of meeting their father even after this came out.

Take care.

Grace

Well, thank you very much Grace! She really needn't have dragged the email out for so long. A couple of sentences would have sufficed.

Hi Cleo,
You're a bitch. We all hate you.

Not in a million years would Mark tell me that Alexander hated me. There was no need. Mark and I had already discussed the boys possible negative reaction towards me and I had said he needed to see them a few times first before I met with them.

The last sentence insinuating that I was the one who was in the way of the boys seeing their father was a bit below the belt. I'd searched for flights and offered to book them for him but there was always an excuse, more often than not a feeble one. The only person in the way of the boys seeing their dad was, ironically, their dad. We argued about it. He could not understand why I was so hell bent on him going to Sweden. When I mentioned Grace's offer of him staying at her house he looked at me as if I had asked him to chop his own dick off. I explained that the sooner it was sorted out the sooner everyone could move on with their lives. He was confused as to what needed sorting. As far as he was concerned it was over. When I mentioned Grace deserving closure his reaction was less than understanding.

'Closure on what for fucks sake? What a load of old bollocks.'

From Cleo
On Oct 26, 2014, at 19:45:

Hi Grace

Had to think things over before I replied to your email so apologies for late reply.
I have spoken to Mark about going to Sweden and him staying with the boys at your home. He does not want to do this as he feels it would be inappropriate given the situation. I think it is a reasonable compromise that I go with him and keep out of the way so he can give the boys his undivided attention. I am sorry they feel the way they do about me but I think it is a normal reaction and I am sure as they get older it will be easier for them to accept me. This is not about me anyway. It's about Mark keeping in contact with his sons. We all have to accept that things will never be as they were. I know you want things to stay as normal as possible but unfortunately that cannot happen. It's not fair but life isn't fair is it, especially when Mark is involved.
As for you getting closure - Mark does not do closure, he walks away - always has and always will.
Your comparison of Mark and an alcoholic is very accurate. If you look at this situation like that, at the moment he is in rehab - detoxifying himself of lies. He is showing me texts you have sent to prove he is not keeping anything from me. Let's hope he makes a successful recovery!!!!
You are right when you say he does not want to hurt anyone

but unfortunately it is inevitable that will happen.

Mark thinks it would be best for the boys to come over here - at least if they stayed at their grandparents that would feel somewhat normal for them.
I have told Mark that he really needs to "man up" and be honest. There is no point in him telling me one thing and telling you something different.
Please let's keep everything civil - there has been enough upset already.
Take care
Cleo

From Grace
On Oct 26 2014 at 22:34:

Hi Cleo!
I didn't really expect an answer from you but I am glad you answered so thank you. I might answer a bit too quickly, especially since I had wine to dinner, but here it comes anyway!

Well - Mark can't walk away from this one, not if he wants to see his sons. I need to speak to him face to face - in London or here. And I'm sorry but I don't think it has been enough upset - maybe you feel that because you've been there and had a chance to deal with it, but I haven't and that is yet to come.
I'm glad that you can see the similarity with an alcoholic. Some of the steps to recover is:

- *making amends for past errors*
- *learning to live a new life with a new code of behaviour*

and right now I can't see that the rehab is working. He still can't say/admit that you are living together (though I know that 99,9% of the population would consider you two as a couple living together - the rest are the mental ones). And trusting him because he shows texts seems a bit naive - it is very easy to delete texts that isn't showing 'the right thing'. Now I understand his strange polite 'thank you' texts that always comes like out of the blue and doesn't connect with what we talk about. No wonder he refused to answer my last text and wanted to call me instead.
You and I have one goal in common, that Mark will "man up", but I don't think neither you or I would consider it manly to be a marionette - acting after a script that you or I have written. He will never 'recover' as long as everyone else around him protects him from bad feelings, makes decisions and handles things for him. Around alcoholics there are always co-dependent loved ones, making the drinking (lies in Marks case) possible.
I'm looking forward to hear what Mark has to say after this weekend. Hopefully with his own words. Take care.
Grace

Fuck me, this woman was like a dog with a bone. She was not going to rest until she had got her pound of flesh from the father of her children and who could blame her. What she failed to realise was, that if Mark was given a choice of not seeing his sons or walking away he would have chosen the latter. He wasn't interested in making amends or changing his behaviour, not as far as that situation was concerned anyway. He just wanted to put it all behind him and move on. He appeared to be focusing all his efforts on repairing our relationship, showing a lot more enthusiasm than I was. We were still at the stage where he wanted to be with me far more than I wanted to be with him. I was happier than I had been for a while but not nearly as happy as I could have been. I was getting a bit fed up of Grace and her snide comments. Mark didn't say he lived with me because he didn't. I used to make that crystal clear every time we argued.

'You only stay here with me, remember that. If we split up you walk out of here with the bag you brought with you and nothing else.'

It didn't help that he once overheard me at a friends party telling a woman I had just been introduced to that I lived on my own and Mark lived with his mum and dad.

And of course it was easy to delete texts but it helped that I had the passwords for all of his devices and his two email addresses including his phone which he left unattended whenever he was with me. If I chose to I could pick it up and check it anytime I liked. Photos sent to his phone went straight to the iPad's we shared. I had gone through a painful break up myself when I was much younger and I knew what it entailed. There is a sense of intimacy in the conversations and communication you have with someone you have been close to when the end is inevitable. There is a need to say things you may never get another chance to. I was okay with that happening between Grace and Mark. If she interpreted my understanding as naivety then so be it. I came home from work one evening to find Mark sitting in the armchair, pale faced and eyes swollen from crying. I asked what was wrong. He told me he'd had a long conversation with Grace and that she'd been great about the situation. I could see it had been emotional and cathartic for him and rather than feel jealous of any closeness they may have shared during the conversation I felt sure it had cleared the air making way for a good co-parenting relationship in the future.

In November Mark surprised me with a five night break in the most delightful Fishermans cottage in Whitby, North Yorkshire. The weather was perfect. Freezing cold, crisp air blowing in our faces as we walked hand in hand along the beautiful beaches as the wind made our eyes water. We ate salt and vinegar soaked fish and chips out of the paper and won the ugliest looking teddy bear I had ever seen in the arcades. I discovered a knitting shop in a village high street that was having a closing down sale and bought over fifty balls of wool and a bagful of patterns. Everything was perfect until the last evening. We had decided to stay in and cook a meal. Mark suggested I take a bath while he got on with the cooking. I came down an hour later to a beautifully laid table, a glass of champagne and a small red box with the distinctive gold pattern at the edges resting in the palm of Marks hand.

'Before you say anything it's not an engagement ring so don't panic 'Mark said.

I reached for the box and opened it. It was the platinum love band to match my bangle. I loved it and shrieked with delight to show my appreciation. The icing on the cake was that it fitted my finger perfectly. How I went from pure joy to dark thoughts in a matter of seconds is beyond me. Up until that moment my mind had been focused on nothing but my immediate surroundings. The tiles in the bathroom that I liked, the smell of the candle flickering at the end of the bath, the feel of the cashmere jumper that slid over my arms as I dressed to go downstairs, the pleasure I felt seeing Mark smile at me.

As I turned my hand checking out the ring on my finger from different angles I asked Mark if he had bought Grace a love band ring in the past.

'Where the hell has that come from? 'he asked clearly puzzled by my question.

'So you have then 'I shouted ripping the ring from my finger and slamming it on the table in front of me.

'No, I haven't Cleo, I promise you'.

'You and your fucking promises 'I screamed.

'Please Cleo, calm down 'pleaded Mark. He moved towards me but I backed away into the living area.

My brain went into overdrive and I couldn't get the words out quick enough.

'All the presents you bought for me, you bought for her as well. The Cartier love bangles, the Tiffany rings and bracelets, the diamond earrings, the diamond and pink sapphire cross, my watches with the engraving on the back. What about the Mulberry bags? Has she got the same Louis Vuitton bags and purses as me?'

I was on a roll reeling off nearly thirteen years worth of gifts.

'When we get back I'm getting rid of them all, every last one of them. They mean nothing to me anymore.'

I stomped back to the table and picked up the ring holding it up to his face.

'Take this and shove it up your lying arse.'

Mark looked truly devastated and suddenly I was overwhelmed by the desire to be in his arms. I threw myself at him and we hugged like we'd never let each other go. I never did find out if Grace was the recipient of identical gifts, nor did I carry out my threat to get rid of all the presents that he had bought me. I may be daft but I'm not stupid.

From Cleo
On Dec 22 2014 at 10:06:

Hi Grace,
How are you?
Hope all is well in Sweden. Just need your advice on when would be the best days for Mark to see the boys. We are looking at booking a weekend probably early Feb. Would it be best to

come over on a Friday leaving on a Sunday or come over on a Saturday and leave on the Monday?
Also, are the boys coming over for the Chelsea game in March?
Apologies if email sounds abrupt (not my intention) rushing round like a headless chicken at the moment trying to get everything done before Christmas.
I know you must be busy but please try and get back to me as I want to book as soon as possible.
Cheers
Cleo

I was still trying my utmost to arrange a visit and could not understand why it hadn't taken place already. Why the hell didn't Grace and the boys just get on a plane to England and call Mark when they landed? Why the hell didn't Mark just get on a plane to Sweden and call Grace when he landed? I thought I had sent a reasonably worded email but it seemed that Grace disagreed. She told Mark I had pissed her off for Christmas amongst other things.

From Grace
On Dec 23 2014 at 20.47

Hi Cleo!
Sorry for sounding abrupt back.
I have told Mark that all he has to do is to tell me that he loves you and wants to spend his life with you and I will make it easy for you to get a relationship with the boys and be part of their life - but he just 'hmms'. Somehow I don't think he wants his two (if that's all) lives to meet. And he still doesn't call it that you and him are living together. This makes it totally awkward for me and the boys that you are coming. I really really can't

understand why he just can't say that he wants to be with you? I couldn't possibly think any less of him. And it makes it hard that he put us in this situation without strong feelings involved. I really would respect him more if he stood by your side and tried to make things work with you and the boys. Hope you come to your senses when it comes to this man - if you do I'd like to meet you, I think we can have fun together!
I can't let you know what's best this early on - weekends don't get planned until late due to Alexander football and other stuff. Mark will have to come with a suggestion to me and I will let him know if it works.
As for the Chelsea game - boys won't come over by themselves before Mark and I have had a talk. And if he doesn't come to Sweden before, then I am going with them to London to talk to him there. And he will pay for a luxury hotel room of my choice.
Cheers,
Grace

To be honest I really could not see what relevance Mark's living arrangements had to do with seeing his sons. Even less relevant was how he felt about me. All Grace needed to know was that he wasn't in love with her. Regardless whether Mark and I loved or hated each other, it had no impact on the feelings he had for his sons. I could read the anger between the lines in Grace's email and a vision of her typing away on her iPad sipping from a Margarita, calling me all manner of bitches came to mind. The time had come for me to stop interfering and offering up suggestions. It wasn't helping the situation, in fact from Grace's point of view it seemed I was making it worse. With Christmas looming and a new year not far away it was time to wave goodbye and say bloody good riddance to quite possibly the worst year of my life. I would leave them to get on with it. They had after all been making arrangements to see each other for the past fifteen years without any help from me whatsoever.

Twenty-four

I made two new year resolutions for 2015.

The first was to acquire a mobile phone.

The second was to start looking after myself. Having a year long nervous breakdown had taken it's toll. I still resembled a lollipop head and I took no pleasure in seeing my hip bones jutting out or my clavicle so prominent. I could have ditched my handbag and put my keys and purse in the pockets created by the lack of fat on my collarbone. I gave up smoking much to Marks delight and that helped with my appetite. Unfortunately alcohol was still my favourite thing on the menu and I was not quite in the right headspace to give it up. Baby steps and all that. I left Mark to get on with the arrangements to see his sons and end the relationship with Grace in a decent manner. Eventually after phone calls, whassaps and texts (most of which I read before before Mark did) a visit was arranged. It was a four night trip in April. The boys would be staying with Mark at his parents in Putney and Grace would book herself into a hotel. As she had pointed out before Mark would be paying and I hoped she was thinking along the lines of the Savoy (superb cocktail list) or the Dorchester (superb wine list).

I accompanied him to the bank where he transferred money into Grace's account ensuring it didn't come out of our joint account. The amount he transferred wouldn't have got her one night in the Savoy or the Dorch. I'm not sure if it was a case of Grace being frugal or Mark being unusually tight-arsed.

She had made it abundantly clear that I was not to meet the boys on their first visit and I agreed without reservation. They were coming over for a long weekend on an early evening flight and Mark was picking them up from the airport. We were both off work on their arrival day and spent it at home pottering around and relaxing. Correction, I was relaxing he was getting more nervous as the hours ticked by.

'Jesus, Mark 'I said as he sat in the chair in the garden, his legs bouncing off the grass like he was in the throes of some sort of fit. 'Carry on like that and you'll have no energy left to pick them up. I'll have to get them and I don't think that would go down too well.'

I was trying to make a joke of it but he wasn't seeing the funny side. Our moods could not have been further apart. I was happy that things were finally going to be sorted with Grace and more importantly he was going to spend time with his sons. I thought it was disgraceful that he hadn't seen them for well over a year. Kissing him goodbye at the door as he left for the airport I told him everything would be fine. I told him not to worry about calling me and just concentrate on his kids.

My phone woke me up at about eleven o'clock that night. I hate late phone calls as they usually mean bad news that cannot wait till the morning to be delivered. It was Mark ringing to say goodnight (an hour too late for me). Before I could ask how the reunion had gone he told me he had dropped Grace off at a hotel in Chelsea (about a five minute walk from my old flat oddly enough). She had some questions for him which he answered. Whether or not he had answered honestly will remain a mystery. I had no interest in what was said. It was a private conversation. An end to one relationship and hopefully the beginning of a new one.

My 'Mark free 'weekend kicked off with a couple of friends going for brunch followed by shopping on Oxford Street. I would have been happy to go home and watch crap on the telly but my friends had other ideas. We ended up doing a Soho pub crawl that lasted until I fell into the back of a cab at two o'clock in the morning. Mark had sent me pictures of himself and Alexander at the Chelsea game. The boy obviously didn't realise the picture was going to be sent to me. I don't think his smile would have been quite that wide if he had known.

I woke the next day feeling like shit. Looking in the mirror confirmed I looked like I felt. Imagine my complete horror when I answered the phone to Mark half an hour later informing me that himself and the boys were on their way over. He suggested we could go to Kingston. I suggested he took them himself and leave me out of it.

'I thought Grace didn't want me to meet them yet 'I whined into the phone.

'She doesn't, but I don't care. The boys want to meet you and I want you to meet them.'

There was an obstinate tone in his voice.

'Are you sure you're not forcing them Mark? 'trying my best to sound assertive.

I knew how forceful he could be. I wanted to meet the boys at the right time for everybody. I'm not sure their first sight of me bleary eyed, hungover and smelling of booze was the right time for me.

In true Mark style he rode roughshod over my protests and announced they would be with me in an hour. One measly hour to transform myself into a woman to rival Julia Roberts in Stepmom.

Fifty nine minutes later and the only thing that even remotely resembled Julia Roberts was perhaps the nail on my little finger.

I need not have worried. As Mark introduced us there were mutual kisses and hugs and I felt comfortable with them straight away. We spent sometime at home just chilling before driving into Kingston, where I managed exceptionally well considering I was suffering from a very sore head and lack of sleep. As I waved them off back to Putney I knew they would be staying at my house in the future. From my point of view my first meeting with them could not have gone any better though I wasn't sure Grace would agree.

I didn't see them again on that first trip. I'm not sure what they did although I thought there was a strong possibility that Mark and the boys would have met up with Grace for a meal at least. I hoped they had as it was important for Lucas and Alexander to see that their parents could still enjoy each others company despite no longer being together. When I explained how I felt to Lisa over a glass of wine in her kitchen she was incredulous at my 'lax attitude 'as she called it.

'You're giving him free rein to do what he likes after all he's put you through 'she spluttered nearly choking on a tortilla chip.

'Lisa, adults do not have reins. They are for animals and small children. I cannot let what has happened change my personality. I've never been a jealous person and I don't plan on turning into one. I think if he was ever going to make a life with Grace it would have happened a long long time ago. What difference does it make to me if they spend time together? Having said that if he calls me to say they've declared undying love for each other over a cheese and bacon burger and he's decided to go back to Sweden with her, you'll be visiting me in Holloway. Category A prisoner, double murder.'

By now Lisa was laughing and topping up our wine glasses.

'I wouldn't put it past you Cleo 'she said.

I need not have worried. The Larsons were dropped off at the airport and Mark came home to me. He was pleased with how the trip had gone and happy he had broken the ice that had formed in the fifteen months he had been apart from his sons. He asked me what I thought of them and I answered truthfully.

'Very nice, well mannered boys. They were a joy to be around. Er, just one thing though. Why do all three of your sons look like they need a blood transfusion? How comes not one of them has your colouring? They don't look anything like you. I'm just saying.'

Mark started laughing.

'Think of the money I'd save if they weren't actually mine.'

'Working on the proviso that Lucas and Alexander are yours you need to get the maintenance payments sorted out' I said being serious.

'Yeah, I'll sort that out with Grace 'he answered casually.

He led me to believe that it would take a phone call between himself and Grace to agree on a fair monthly amount in keeping with the upbringing of two teenage boys. It seemed her mention of the Swedish authorities had gone by the wayside and she was happy to sort it out between herself and Mark.

My days of checking Mark's mobile were short-lived. Unless him and Grace were making plans to run off together it was of no consequence to me what they were communicating about. I certainly wasn't interested in messages from Grace reminding Mark how many times she had mopped the boys brows when they had been sick or how many loads of laundry she had done for them over the years. Attaching photographic evidence of Alexander lying on his bed with a pained expression on his face and a wet flannel on his forehead whilst suffering from a headache was just a touch too dramatic for me.

On a brighter note a trip had been arranged for the boys to come over unchaperoned by their mother in August. In the week leading up to it I concentrated on getting the house ready for our Swedish guests by going shopping in Ikea for a spare bed, meatballs and cinnamon buns.

Considering the circumstances that had brought the boys to my house instead of Putney, their first visit went extremely well. The meatballs remained in the freezer untouched as we ate out every day.

It was very much a 'yes' trip for the boys. Wherever they wanted to go, whatever they wanted to eat, drink, do and see, it was a 'yes'. We went to watch Chelsea play at Stamford bridge which was probably more enjoyable for Alexander as he loved football. Lucas got his own back when we went shopping which he was very good at. Mark's wallet was considerably lighter by the end of our shopping expedition.

We drove to Brighton for the day. The sun shone on us as we strolled along the pier eating chips followed by ice cream and crepes. We worked off our recently accumulated calories playing Air Hockey and winning what seemed like five thousand tokens on the arcade machines which we exchanged for, wait for it. No, not a fifty two inch flat screen TV, not a Bose sound system or even a coffee percolator. Our tokens got us a box of stale fudge and a fridge magnet.

On the Sunday Alexander requested a home cooked roast dinner as it had been one of his favourite meals cooked by Elaine on previous trips. I might have been a bit hesitant about dishing up a roast knowing that it would be compared to Elaine's but I had tasted her cooking over the years and let me tell you, Delia Smith had nothing to worry about. The Sunday lunch was a success as was the whole trip and we promised the boys we would see them again before the year was out.

One morning a few days after the boys had gone home Mark and I were lying in bed drinking tea, on our iPads and listening to the radio. I checked my emails and was surprised to see one from Grace. It had been months since I had heard from her. I assumed it would be about the boys recent visit. You know what happens when you assume, right?

I gasped as I read the first line.

Hi,
Congratulations on your anniversary, one year solo after sharing your man with..........

That was as far as I got before slamming the iPad cover over the screen. Of course it was the eleventh of August, a year to the day Grace had opened the email from me that went on to change so many lives.

Mark asked what was up.

'An email from you know who congratulating me on the one year anniversary of having you all to myself. I couldn't bring myself to read the rest so I could be missing out on more heartfelt and warm words 'I added sarcastically.

'She's a fucking bitch 'Mark declared shaking his head.

Why would she be trying to upset me just days after her sons had stayed in my house? What was the point? There wasn't one and neither was there any point in reading the rest of her spiteful email. I lifted the cover fully intending to press the delete button. But before I did, certain words jumped off of the screen at me.

Writing a book/blog .... highlighted links........in English.........so everyone there will know ....lovey dovey pictures on Facebook just to hurt me...... not allowing Mark to go to Sweden.

Unfortunately I am a very quick reader and even as I deleted the email I knew that most of it had been committed to my memory and I would have difficulty in forgetting those words.

Vowing to put all thoughts of Grace out of my mind I got out of bed and went downstairs to make bacon sarnies. She stayed out of it for a couple of weeks until Mark mentioned her name. Apparently she didn't like the fact that Mark and I had celebrated our birthdays at the Landmark Hotel in London. I had posted a couple of pictures on Facebook which was obviously how she knew. Why was she looking at my account anyway? She was in contact with Mark, if she wanted to know what he was doing why didn't she just ask him? I had used Facebook as a tool to help me uncover Mark's secret life. Once I found out about Grace there was no need for me to check her Facebook. I was beginning to see another side to this lady. Mark referred to her as 'The woman scorned 'and up until that point I had always defended her, impressed by the way she had handled things so calmly. I know I would have been a hell of a lot more vocal not to mention physical. It seemed that the old adage 'time is a great healer 'did not apply to Grace. Instead she had been using the time to let her anger stew and simmer gently until the heat was turned up and the lid came off.

To formalise maintenance payments Grace had gone through Försäkingskassan, the Swedish Social Insurance Agency. Mark received a letter from them explaining Grace was applying for maintenance support with a suggested amount each month. He had until September eleventh to dispute the amount which he had no intention of doing. It was reasonable and Mark was happy to agree. So while it was roses round the doorway and skipping through the daisies for Mark and I, Grace decided to pull the rug from under us with an email sent at the end of September.

Subject; Suggested Agreement

Agreement between **Grace Larson** (mother) and

Mark Palmer (father)

Regarding children (hereby referred to as 'the boys');

Lucas Larson and **Alexander Larson**

Mark agrees to, until the month Lucas and Alexander turns 18 (or 20 if still studying or are unemployed and living with their mother):

- Pay a monthly allowance in advance to Grace, the same amount as the minimum amount stipulated by Försäkringskassan (FK) regarding child support. Never less than 100 GBP per child (but more if FK raises the sum and/or the GBP is worth less than 12,75SKR)
- Put extra money of his own choice for the boys directly into their own accounts
- Send presents/gifts for the boys from him exclusively if he wants to (ex. Christmas/birthdays)
- Make sure that he (Mark) and the boys meet at a minimum 3 different occasions every year: 1 in Stockholm*, 1 in London and 1 of Mark's choice
- Pay full amount for these trips for the boys and himself (flights, accommodation, living expenses)
- Take one holiday trip (1 week)** with the boys a year in other place than London or Stockholm and pay for it in full (flights, accommodation, living expenses)
- Pay for all expenses for the boys driving licences (lessons, permits, tests)

*should Mark not come to Stockholm he will pay for at least one trip to London in full per year (flight and a 4-star hotel of Grace's choice) for Grace and the boys
**should Mark not take the boys on the holiday trip he will pay Grace for half the boys cost of a 2-week or 2 x 1-week holiday a year (flight, food and 4-star hotel)

Grace agrees to, until the month Lucas and Alexander turn 18 (or 20 it they are still studying or are unemployed) and are living with her:

- Provide for the boys living expenses in Sweden:

- Food (breakfast, lunch, dinner) and basic clothing

- House (maintenance, electricity, basic furniture)

- Take care of:

- Cleaning, washing

- Garden

- Birthday presents and Christmas gifts

- Pay for Sports activities (fees, cups, trips, basic equipment) and school trips

- Medicine

- Insurance (boys and house)

- Broadband, television, phone (landline and mobiles)

- Transportation costs (subway, bus, cab, train)

- Give them additional driving practice

- Pay a monthly sum of savings for the boys which they can use after they turn 18

Place and date,

____

Our first reaction after reading the agreement was to pick our jaws up off the floor before bursting into slightly hysterical laughter.

I scrolled down the page expecting to read something along the lines of: 'Had you there for a minute didn't I? Who says Swedes haven't got a sense of humour? 'ending with lots of laughing face emoji's.

Mark and I kept passing the iPad backwards and forwards

between each other reading bits out that we just couldn't get our heads around. In the past Grace had called Mark pathetic and here she was dictating that Mark could only send gifts to the boys that were exclusively from him. Pot and kettle came to mind. And why on earth would Grace want to come to London for a holiday let alone getting Mark to pay for it. I was surprised not to see toilet paper and condoms on her list of items she would be providing for her sons. I called her a cheeky bitch which was very subtle compared to the horrendous names Mark called her. He decided there and then that he was having nothing to do with the agreement. They could take him to court if they liked, he couldn't give a shit.

I managed to calm him down and armed with a highlighter pen we put a line through all the things we were not happy with. I typed up our version and sent it to Grace. She sent one back that we still didn't agree with. And so it went on with revised agreements pinging backwards and forwards between us. I was adding no text to the emails but Grace couldn't resist her little digs. When she realised I was involved in sorting out the agreement she asked 'Have you become his secretary now?'

I was so so tempted to send an email back saying 'Yeah, we're playing offices. I'm sitting here in my five inch stiletto heels, mini skirt and blazer with my big tits busting out of my black lacy bra which match my crotchless knickers and my stockings and suspenders. My glasses are perched on the end of my nose, my lips are painted red and my hair is in a neat bun which any moment now Mark is going to release so he can grab handfuls of my hair as he takes me from behind over the kitchen worktop.'

But I held my tongue or rather my fingers and typed nothing.

Twenty-five

Finally in December of that year Mark signed an agreement. It was about fifty lines shorter than the first one and not nearly so ridiculous. I do believe it was the unreasonable suggestions in the first few drafts that pissed Mark off and led to the disintegration of his relationship with Grace. He may have been looking for an excuse to cease all contact and if it wasn't that he would have found another reason. If I could have offered any consolation to Grace to make her feel better it would have been not to take it personally. Quite impossible to do but it was the only way to look at the situation as far as Mark was concerned. It really wasn't personal. He did not continue relationships in any shape or form with people who no longer figured in his life.

I asked several times over the years why this particular behavioral trait did not apply to me and his answer was always the same. 'Because you're different from everyone else '(lucky me - not).

I thought it was sad that two adults who had once been in love and had created two children no longer had anything nice left to say to each other. All Mark could do from that point on was to make sure his relationship with his sons kept growing and moving forward. On the subject of relationships I could not believe the new and wonderful direction ours was taking.

Everything seemed to be falling into place. As Mark was discovering how good it was to lead a virtually stress free life, his anger issues all but vanished. He still displayed his volatile side to others occasionally but around me he was like a Labrador puppy. The last time he had shown any real aggression towards me had been in the August of 2014 just before I had contacted Grace. To this day (nearly six years later) he has barely raised his voice let alone his hand. I wish

I could say the same for myself but I can't. I struggled with my anger issues for a while longer than he did but I'm happy to report that nowadays I keep my fiery side in check with meditation (not to be confused with medication!), walking, swimming and gardening.

As we saw in the New Year I took a few moments to reflect on the last twelve months and how far we had come. I also gave a thought to Grace and the boys mentally crossing my fingers wishing them good things for 2016. I was unsure of how arrangements would be made for the boys trips in that coming year. Grace had made it clear she didn't want to correspond with me, but if she was expecting Mark to arrange flights she needed to tell her boys they would be in for a long wait.

I was relieved to receive an email from Grace in February which opened up the lines of communication between us again.

From Grace
On Feb 18 2016 at 08.06
Subject: Alexander is playing a cup in Denmark this Summer

The cup is in the last weekend of July just outside Copenhagen if you would like to come and see him play.
I'm not sure I can go myself and it would be nice if there's someone there to cheer for him. Last time Mark saw him play was 3,5 years ago when he was here with Harry, and for 3 years now Alexander has been playing for another team and has gotten a place in their first team. It is a shame that his dad hasn't seen him play once in it. He needs his support. Maybe this Summer will be a good opportunity for both of you, since he definitely will play and there will be several games during

the (3?) days.

Regards,
Grace

(Please take this as an olive branch, a peace offer. I know that I can't blame you for acting insensitive (in my eyes and in my perspective), but more the blame is Mark's for playing us the way he did, both in the past and after the revelation. It is not you - it is me :-)

(Or you can throw this in the bin)

From Cleo
On Feb 18 2016 at 17.27

Hi Grace,

Olive branch accepted on 2 conditions: It's the biggest branch on the tree and I can smash Mark over the head with it!!! Joking aside, Denmark sounds like a great idea. Let me know the details and I'll get something booked.

On another note, you explained in your last email that the reason you were blogging/writing about this situation was because I wouldn't allow Mark to go to Sweden. I need to put you straight about that. In fact it was the complete opposite. I tried everything I could to persuade him to go; firstly on his own but he was adamant that I go with him. Then I tried to

arrange a trip for both of us but he kept coming up with feeble excuses. In the end I gave up. There was no point. I think we both know that Mark only ever does what HE wants when HE wants. I could neither prevent nor enforce him to go to Sweden.
I decided not to click on any of the links you sent me. I felt that as you weren't writing with the "facts intact" as it were, it wouldn't be a true interpretation of what actually happened. You can write honestly from your point of view but you can only make assumptions fuelled by an unreliable source (namely Mark) about my part in it. You may see my refusal to read your work as a form of denial but I can assure you denial doesn't figure in my life. It would be so easy for me to listen to Mark's version of events and believe them.
He is clearly not familiar with Shakespeare

The **man** *doth protest too much methinks*

(I'm tough, I can take it :-)
As for me going on Facebook to hurt you. Not my intention at all. You have to understand Grace, I used Facebook as a means to an end and what a Grand Finale it was! I haven't looked at yours since this all came out. Why would I? In fact I'm coming off of it. I have about 78 friend requests waiting for conformation on there and some of the people I've never even heard of. A couple of nurse's at work have been Facebook stalked by patients and the police have been involved. There's nutter's out there for sure!
One more thing, would it be possible for you to send a list of the boys school holidays so we can arrange for them to come over?

Cheers
Cleo

It was still very important to me that Grace understood that I wasn't standing in the way of Mark going to Sweden. When the shit first hit the fan I was pretty sure that she knew Mark well. However as time passed and her expectations of him came to light I wondered if she ever really knew him at all. If she did she would know he would have no desire to go back to the scene of his crimes. I can only imagine the performance Mark had put on when in the company of his Swedish fam. I'm sure the mask slipped a few times but for the most part I'm sure he portrayed himself as charm personified. If I read her book/blog I could find out more about his behaviour but why would I bother. I had no interest in the past. I hated history lessons at school and when a friend bought me a subscription to a genealogy website as a birthday gift I asked if she could get a refund. I'm all for the present and the future where there is possibility, potential, hope and optimism. The past is best left where it belongs. Behind us. If writing about her relationship with Mark helped her move on then good luck to her. There were far worse things that ex-partners did to each other.

I was just happy to be back in contact.

Grace did as I asked and sent me a detailed list of the boys availability throughout the coming year. She was clearly very organised which I liked. I too was an organiser by nature and my nickname amongst friends was 'The leader'. I could have taken my moniker to insinuate I was bossy and I couldn't argue with that.

Grace made it clear that everything had to be cleared by her first before booking any flights. She also made it clear by her closing sentence that she was far from impressed with Mark's recent fathering skills.

Might have forgotten something, but here is the big picture. Remind Mark that he hasn't seen his boys for 7 months.

Regards,

Grace

Between Grace, myself and Mark's debit card we managed to arrange three trips for the boys that year. I was mindful of the agreement that Mark had signed and booking in advance early on in the year allowed me to breathe easy as well as bagging bargain flights.

Communication between Grace and I was light and easy going focused mainly around school holidays and travel arrangements. She referred to Mark as 'Dickhead 'if she ever needed to mention him, but not in a nasty way. As much as I loved him I could not bring myself to defend him or disagree with her choice of name.

I should have learnt from past experience that when all seemed well in my world something usually came along to upset the apple cart.

The something in question was an email from Grace.

From Grace
On 11 September 2016, at 06:37

Hi Cleo! I hope everything is alright with you.
I'm coming to London Saturday - Tuesday, October 1st-4th - want to meet up for a drink (or two)? I'll be busy on the Sunday from about three o'clock with a book-signing at The White Horse on Parson's Green, which you (and Mark) are welcome to of course, but other than that I'm free.
Or maybe I can come to your house and see where the boys

now are staying while they're over, feels like enough time has passed :-) You can make sure that Mark is out of the house, or not - depending on what you are comfortable with. Lucas is talking about moving over to his dad when he finishes school, which I am totally okay with, but of course I'd like to see where he is going to stay.

My book is now published and available as an e-book at Apple iBooks among other sites. It is possible to read a sample there. If you want a signed, printed book you have to come to the book-signing, they are only able to order from Sweden right now. Or if you finally want to see Stockholm I'm having a release-party on Wednesday September 21st - you (with or without Mark) are more than welcome!

At the end of the book I have written an acknowledgement to you, where I'm trying to explain the mixed emotions when it comes to you :-)

Of course I was hoping for something else when it came to me Mark until I found out about you, but when I did - I'm glad it's you. You seem like a nice and fun person. You deserve better than Mark and he doesn't deserve you, but apart from that I think you have acted great, especially when it comes to the boys.

Why have I written this book? Because Mark wouldn't 'man up 'about the situation he put us in. He could have lifted his arse and flown over to Stockholm and ended it with me in a proper and decent way. Now - Karma will hit him in the head. (And maybe me too, but I think that I have been fair enough in the book). All the names are changed, and I'm publishing it under the name Andrea Hunter.

It is called 'Too Good to be True - or How I met your father'.

I hope we can meet. I totally understand if you are not comfortable with it, but I hope we can talk and laugh about everything, and put things behind us and move forward.

Let me know your thoughts.
Grace

I read and re-read the email several times searching for the sarcasm hidden between the lines. Surely she wasn't extending a genuine invitation to Mark and actually expecting him to turn up. Wild horses could not have dragged him to that pub.

I was surprised she was bothering to come to London in the first place although I remembered she had mentioned before she was writing it in English so everyone over here would know what he had done. I wasn't sure who she was referring to. Everyone over here had known what was going on (apart from me, obviously). I assumed she would be inviting Elaine and Paul and John and Kerry. Was she expecting me to clink glasses and make idle chit chat over copies of a book that hopefully exposed their true colours. I would rather have had my fingernails pulled out followed by wisdom tooth extraction minus anaesthetic than spend a moment with those connivers. What did she think she was going to achieve by lifting the lid on Mark and his deviousness? If she was attempting to make him feel guilty or ashamed she was wasting her time. Mark could not care less about what others thought of him.

I wished her well and hoped it was a success but I wanted no part of it. Having said that, I knew without a doubt that if we met we would get on. There would be so many people to slag off, so many notes to compare, so much alcohol to consume. I felt sure another opportunity would arise in the future and I would know if the time was right.

From Cleo
On 16 September 2016, at 07:56

Hi Grace,

Sorry for the delay in replying. Took a while to gather my thoughts!

I'm busy on the weekend you are over. At a charity event on the Saturday, working on the Sunday and Monday.
Even if I had been available I wouldn't have come to the book signing. As I have pointed out to you before I have no desire to read it. Not then, not now, nor in the future. It has the potential to hurt people that don't deserve the pain. I would hate to think of Mark's ex-wives finding out about it. Can you imagine how Harry's Mum would feel knowing that her son has been keeping secrets from her for so many years. Contrary to what Mark may have said about her, she is actually a nice lady who was fortunate enough to escape Mark's clutches! As for his second wife - she would be heartbroken.
You have your reason for writing it which I understand. But come on, using words like proper and decent in the same sentence as Mark - that would be like seeing Mother Teresa and weapons of mass destruction in the same sentence!

I hope you get the closure? satisfaction? peace? you are looking for.
Hope all goes well at your party and book-signing. Have a glass of champagne for me ;-)

Cheers
Cleo

From Grace
On 16 September 2016, at 08.49

Thank you for your reply! I respect your thoughts about the book and the book-signing. You don't have to read it of course! Although I hope you would rethink about having a drink with me when I come over. If you change your mind get in touch. If it suits you better I can come when the boys are coming later in October.

When it comes to his ex-wives I have a different opinion than you. Second wife probably lived in as much frustration and questions as me, and getting an explanation gives a feeling of satisfaction, even if time has passed. Does wonders for the self confidence. As for Harry's mum Mark has assured me that she knows about the boys. No more secrets. He wanted Harry to tell her (coward) and then he told me that she already had known for some time. I wouldn't have let the boys over on their own the first time last Summer if he hadn't told me that she knew - and if he lied about that too, well shame on him. She will get the book. If he hasn't told her by now he has to be quick.

Despite what Mark has told you about me, I am not mad ;-) , but I just don't like to be treated like this, without him handling it in a decent way, and then being ignored on top of that. I'm still the mother of two of his sons.
The boys will get all the profit from the book, if any, by the way.

As I have said before - I like you, and I wish you well. I will definitely have a glass of champagne for you, and a couple of Margaritas :-)

All the best!
(and I really would like to meet you - you seem fun, nice and cool :-)

Grace

I pushed all thoughts of Grace and her book to the back of my mind. It was only when I was filling in a form at work and wrote 03/10/16 in the date box did I remember she was in London. I happened to be working on a session collecting blood in a hall in Fulham. I had a sudden urge to email Grace and tell her to meet me on Putney Bridge at eight o'clock that night. I was due a break so I made myself a coffee, grabbed my phone and deliberated what to type. Had I not given it so much thought and taken so long Grace and I may have met that night. As it was I had only typed 'Hi Grace 'when I was called back to the floor to deal with a very irate donor who had been waiting for over an hour to be seen. I never got another chance to send an email so maybe it just wasn't meant to be.

The boys were due over towards the end of that month which we were looking forward to. The other occasion we had to look forward to that October was the fifty fourth wedding anniversary of Elaine and Paul. Mark had persuaded me to book a table at a restaurant we liked, overlooking Epsom Downs. I say persuaded as making arrangements and doing things for Mark's parents did not come naturally to me following the revelations of 2014. The thought of the sticky toffee pudding and custard I would be ordering for my dessert and the wine Paul and I would knock back made the thought of our lunch bearable.

I needn't have worried about it. We never even stepped outside the house. As we were getting ready for our celebratory lunch Mark was drying himself after his shower and put his foot up on the edge of the bath to dry his lower leg. In doing so he managed to put his back out. I was getting ready in the bedroom just about to put my underwear on when I heard him yell my name. Running into the bathroom and seeing his face completely drained of colour I thought he was having a heart attack. I ran back to the bedroom to get his GTN spray realising on my return that his hand was pressing on his lower back, and was not in fact clutching his heart.

'Cleo, it's my back, I can't move.'

I took his hands and rested them on my shoulders.

'Lean on me and walk slowly towards me so we can get you to the bedroom.'

He tried to put one foot in front of the other but I could see the pain etched across his face and hear the sharp intake of breath when he moved.

'Grip my shoulders and shuffle 'I said. 'You'll have to bear the pain till you get on the bed.'

Under normal circumstances the pair of us stark naked making our way to our bedroom would have ended up very pleasurably. Not on this occasion.

By the time Elaine and Paul knocked on the door half an hour later Mark was lying awkwardly on the bed groaning in pain and I was slipping into my jeans.

'Mark's put his back out 'I explained as they came through the door.

'My back's been playing me up something terrible lately.

You just have to get on with it.'

This from Elaine who could not be out done in the pain or illness stakes.

Paul went straight upstairs to see him whilst Elaine complained the stairs were too steep for her and proceeded to make herself comfortable on the sofa.

I made some tea and we chatted about nothing in particular. Quite suddenly Elaine's demeanour changed. With a glance towards the staircase she shuffled forward to the edge of her seat and spoke in a hushed conspiratorial tone.

'Grace came to see me when she was in London. She left copies of the book she has written for you and Mark but I didn't bring them over just in case.'

She jerked her head upwards, raising her eyebrows, informing me silently that the 'just in case 'applied to Mark.

'Quite honestly Elaine, neither of us want anything to do with it so if you wouldn't mind disposing of our copies however you see fit.'

I was hoping Elaine would pick up on the finality with which my words were spoken but alas she was on a roll and it appeared there was no stopping her.

'She paid for everything you know, getting the books printed, her book party and coming to London. I don't think it was cheap either. She can't understand how you're still with Mark. Say's you deserve better.'

She paused to take a sip of tea before continuing.

'She say's she will always love him 'she said, a wistful tone to her voice.

Now, I could have been wrong but I got the distinct impression she was trying to wind me up and she was enjoying it.

I'd had enough. It was one thing to recall the conversation but quite another to repeat comments not meant for me.

'Right 'I said with a clap of my hands. 'I'm off upstairs to see how the patient's doing, then we'll see what to do about something to eat.'

Experience should have taught me that Elaine would never let anyone have the last word. As I took away our empty cups and saucers she said in less hushed tones than before.

'I've started reading it you know. So far all it's about is her spreading her legs 'she said distastefully.

It was on the tip of my tongue to say 'Jealous are you?'

Knowing she was going to be in my home for the next few hours and not wanting to create an atmosphere I refrained from making my comment. Instead I checked on Mark who was watching football with his dad lying next to him on the bed. I felt like asking if there was room for one more. I wasn't in the mood to be sociable, all I wanted to do was look after Mark, watch my favourite film of all time 'A Star is Born ' (Barbra Streisand/Kris Kristofferson version) and have a glass of wine. My drinking (or lack of it) was much more under control by then and I was able to enjoy a glass or two rather than drink the whole bottle before opening a second one.

There was not enough food in the house for me to knock up a meal with so I gave Elaine a handful of take-away menus. She chose a curry which I ate at the kitchen table with the in-laws while Mark ate his off of a tray in bed trying hard not to spill chicken dhansak over the clean white bedding I had put on earlier that morning.

The next day we managed to get Mark to an osteopath where it was confirmed he had slipped a disc. There was nothing more he could do apart from rest and dose himself up with painkillers neither of which he liked doing. The boys were due over a couple of weeks later and we seriously considered cancelling the trip. It wouldn't be much fun for them if their dad spent the whole time lying on the sofa or in bed.

Thankfully as each day passed the pain lessened and movement returned. The boys came over as planned and the third and final trip of 2016 was yet another pleasurable event for all concerned.

Twenty-six

2017 kicked off with Mark undergoing a total left knee replacement. It was yet another part of his body that had failed to escape damage from his rugby playing days. The consultant had been reluctant to carry out the procedure due to Mark's relatively young age. Most recipients of new knees are usually in their seventies. The up side of Mark being a younger patient meant that he was able to recover and mobilise far quicker. He had the operation on the Thursday morning and I brought him home two days later. He healed like a dog and was the most easy going patient I have ever had to look after. When he was back on his feet and able to exercise we began taking early walks around our local park most mornings before work. That inspired him to embrace a more healthy approach to his diet. There was no denying he had a massive appetite and I cooked accordingly. If anyone saw what I took out of the oven for a mid-week meal they could be forgiven for thinking I was hosting a dinner party for six people.

We limited ourselves to red meat and chicken once a week going meat free for the other five nights. Instead of roasting 2kg of potatoes in goose fat to accompany our Sunday joint I dry roasted two potatoes each. It near enough broke my heart putting a plate of food in front of him that wasn't spilling over the sides and piled up high but he got used to it and the pounds dropped off. He knew his regime would go out the window when the boys came over. Their diet consisted of burgers, pizza's, chips, crisps and chocolate when they were with us and Mark was fully expecting to put on a few of the pounds he had lost when they came over in April. They had already messaged in advance to say they wanted to go Five Guy's.

A week or so before they were due to arrive Mark received

a phone call informing him that due to Alexander's football commitments he would be unable to come over. He had a very important game that he did not want to miss. Although it was disappointing Mark understood and as I pointed out to him it would be good to spend time with Lucas on his own. Mark told Alexander he would try to get something booked so he could come over on his own before their next planned trip in August. I emailed Grace to let her know I would try to get a flight booked and she replied the same day.

From Grace
On 27 April 2017 at 11.53

Hi Cleo
If you can't book anything for Alexander this spring maybe it is time for you to come and see him (and Lucas) in Stockholm instead? Alexander really wants his father to see him play a game in his current team. If you come here we don't have to worry about what's on at school and in football. It is not fair on the boys that they have to do all the traveling just to be able to meet their dad.
Have a nice weekend and take good care of my soon-to-be-18-big boy :-D
Grace

I had to hand it to this lady. She was persistent. She was also thick skinned. It did not appear to be sinking in that Mark had no desire to visit Stockholm. For him I think it was a case of 'Been there, done that, bought the t-shirt'. (And he'd done a lot more than just buying the t-shirt).

From Cleo
On 27 April 2017 at 15.27

Hi Grace,
Flights booked for those dates in August, travel documents to follow.

It is not looking good for a visit before August for Alexander.
With commitments on both sides it's probably not possible.
As for us coming to Stockholm..............?
Looking forward to Lucas's arrival tomorrow although we are disappointed the footballer won't be with him! Personally I think that level of dedication is to only be admired.
Wish him luck for his game x
Rest assured Lucas will be taken good care of.
Cleo

Grace's reply to me was chatty and familiar, cleverly getting her point across in a friendly manner referring to one particular line in my last email. As for us coming to Stockholm............?

I wondered what ....? meant.
'You have got to be kidding.....?', 'Are you mad.......?', 'Only time will tell....?', 'Maybe......?', 'Are we welcome......?', 'Who knows.......?', 'If I can make dickhead to move his fat arse and get his finger out.....? 'or other :-)
I think both yourself and the boys deserve you and Mark visiting Stockholm. Or maybe you should come without dickhead if he is too scared, too busy, too avoiding or too lazy ;)

I got both emails with August trip for both boys by the way. Thanks for arranging it!

Have a lovely weekend, and may the force be with Alexander so they win this game!

Say hello to di... Mark for me please.

Grace

Did I email back and tell her she was flogging a dead horse? Should I let her live in hope that one day Mark might change his mind and meet the boys in Stockholm? I knew that Mark would do anything for me and if I really really pushed for it, using all my powers of persuasion I could get him there. But what would be the point. A father spending time with his children was a supposedly happy occasion. Doing it under duress would not make for a good time. As far as Mark was concerned there were two options open for his son's. Come to England or don't.

Sadly the August trip was less of a success than previous ones had been. Both boys seemed distracted and slightly bored. Much to Mark's annoyance they spent a lot of time speaking to each other in Swedish. Paranoia set in and he convinced himself they were talking about him. We asked them if they were okay, if they were enjoying themselves, was there anything they wanted to do? Their impeccable manners would not allow them to give rude answers. I think there was a feeling of relief all round when they went home. To compound matters, a couple of weeks later a letter arrived from Försäkringskassan, the agency dealing with the maintenance payments. I opened it to read the following:

This letter is being sent to you because Lucas Larson has submitted an application for extended maintenance support.

It went on to explain the information that Lucas had given them to support his claim. Mark had already agreed to pay maintenance until both boys were twenty as long as they were living at home and in full time education. It seemed pointless to claim for something he was already receiving. It was obviously a formality due to the fact Lucas had turned eighteen and was still at school. Had I not left the letter on the kitchen worktop instead of putting it in the file I kept for such correspondence Mark would have been none the wiser. As it was he glanced over at it as we were eating lunch later that day. He very nearly choked on his salt beef and gherkin bagel as his eyes behind his reading glasses flew over the page.

'What the fuck's all this about? Are they trying to get more money out of me now? 'His voice rising with each question.

'Calm down 'I said taking the letter off of him and pointing to the amount. 'It's what he's already getting. Försäkringkassan probably contacted him and told him he had to fill the form in, just a case of dotting the i's and crossing the t's'.

Mark would not be pacified with my explanation's. Grabbing his phone he scrolled through his contacts until he came to Lucas. Before I had a chance to say 'wait 'I heard the phone connect. Not one to beat about the bush (in certain situations at least) Mark launched his attack as soon as his son said 'Hello'.

I took myself into the front room with my cup of tea and the newspapers not wanting to get involved. I couldn't help but hear the conversation was not going that well. I heard Mark end the call only for his phone to start ringing not a minute later. This time it was Grace attempting to explain the situation. She had no more luck than her son did and clearly not wanting to be on the receiving end of Mark's abuse she put the phone down on him cutting him off mid sentence.

Before he could start ranting about that I reminded him of his half eaten bagel.

'Come and finish your lunch, it took me ages to cook that beef 'I said.

'Pass me the mustard please 'he said as he sat back down at the table and resumed eating.

What a wonderful pacifier food was.

I learnt a lesson that day. Never leave letters lying around on the kitchen worktop especially if they were from Sweden asking for money. I would be glad when dealings with the Försäkringskassan were over. That would happen when the boys left full time education or turned twenty, which ever came first. Judging by their responses when asked how school was going I was confident they would be leaving as soon as they could. Alexander had aspirations of becoming a footballer whilst Lucas was apparently going to be a millionaire by the time he was twenty-five though how he was going to achieve that remained undecided.

Mark was also giving thought to his future, career wise. As fit and strong as he was there was no getting away from the facts that he had a heart condition and he wasn't getting any younger. He still classed himself as a builder and even though he wasn't on the tools regularly he still liked to keep his hand in. His heart consultant had warned him against lifting heavy objects and over exerting himself, difficult to adhere to when building a back extension or a loft conversion on a tight schedule. That September an opportunity for a complete change of direction came from an unlikely source.

Many years ago I had gone out with a guy called Lee. He was the warmest, kindest man I had ever met and so funny he used to make me cry with laughter. Ingredients for a great relationship one might think. My ever perceptive mother hit the nail on the head when we were discussing relationships one night over dinner.

'He's lovely 'I said referring to Lee 'but I don't think it's going to last with him 'I added, expecting her to be shocked by this admission.

'Course it's not going to last. He's far too nice for you. You need someone to take you down a peg or two not keep putting you on a pedestal.'

Thanks for that mum. She did actually love me despite what comments like that may lead people to believe. It was my call to split up and he was devastated. However because he had always been such a good friend to me I never really lost touch with him. He had gone on to meet a woman who sat quite happily on the pedestal he put her on and they adored each other equally. I decided to bite the bullet and told Mark I was thinking of inviting Lee and Clare for dinner sometime. He raised an eyebrow but agreed if a little reluctantly. He did not agree with keeping in touch with ex's and didn't think I should either. If he had said no and I hadn't gone ahead with that dinner party our lives would be very different today. They clicked from the moment they met as I knew they would. Their friendship developed over the years and it was Lee who came to Mark with a business proposition. He wanted him to manage a waste company that he had just acquired. Mark was thrown in at the deep end and proved himself far beyond expectations. He worked really hard and we were proud of him.

We had finally reached the stage where we were "living our best lives". We lived a perfectly contented simple existence. We went to work, came home, shopped, cooked, took drives to the country, drives to the coast, exercised, made love, talked, debated, tended to the garden, drank wine at night round the fire pit, held hands in the street, held hands in bed, got on planes to sunny places, stayed in cottages in cold places, danced to soul music in the kitchen and laughed a lot. We amazed ourselves at how much we loved each other. I asked him once how he thought his life might have turned out if we had separated in 2014.

'I wouldn't have let us separate. I would have hounded you for about six months until you gave in.'

'But what about if I was somehow able to resist your undeniable charm? 'I joked.

'I would have gone completely off my head and committed murder. I would have spent the rest of my days rotting in a prison cell giving Charles Bronson a run for his money 'he joked back.

Best all round that we stayed together then, I thought to myself as I watched him pruning one of the Maple's in our garden. How could a man whose mind held such thoughts of violence be capable of holding a delicate leaf with such gentleness and respect for nature. At times he was a mystery to me although he always insisted I knew him better than he knew himself. When it came to his body I agreed with that. It was as familiar to me as my own. I knew every part of him from the ridges on his toenails to the scar on his head inflicted by me aiming a heavy glass candle at him during one of our heated discussions. We had been loving every inch of each others bodies for nearly two decades and I prayed for at least three more.

PART THREE

Secrets Made

Twenty-seven

In February of this year Mark and I celebrated eighteen years together. I would like to say eighteen HAPPY years but I'm not one to kid myself. A couple of them were diabolical while a few were hard work. Some tested patience, some tested our love. For a while there our boat had sailed through stormy waters, tossed about while we hung on for dear life, so close to being lost at sea. I'm so grateful we finally found our safe harbour.

Although it was early in the year we had already made some plans. We were off to Mexico in March for our winter sun holiday. I had booked flights for Lucas and Alexander to visit us in May. This year, for a change of scenery, we wanted to book a cottage by the coast when they came over. In June we had booked an amazing villa overlooking the Aegean Sea in Greece. I had started a new job working in a clinic in London, taking blood, platelets and plasma. It was interesting and varied and I enjoyed the interaction with the donors. I only worked three days a week which left me ample free time to do as I pleased.

But sometimes doing as you please is not all it's cracked up to be. There's only so many lengths you can swim at the pool or times you can walk round the park. There's a limit to the amount of unwanted crap you can buy from Primark or how many times you rearrange your front room furniture. Even meeting friends for lunch lost its appeal if repeated too often. My life was so settled I wanted just a touch of drama to keep me on my toes.

Talk about be careful what you wish for...........

A few days after our anniversary dinner Mark came home from work early. He rang me when he was ten minutes away asking if I could run him a bath. Our days of having baths together although not over were certainly not as frequent as they had once been. I wasn't complaining. There was a subtitled French series I was watching and it was reaching its climactic episode. While he was having a soak I could find out 'qui l'a fait'. He looked shattered when he walked in the door, stripping off his dirty clothes as soon as he could, putting his wallet and phone in the bowl on the console table before making his way upstairs. I promised to bring him up a nice glass of red and a bowl of nibbles. As I poured the wine for us (only fair for me to have a glass of wine whilst watching a French programme) Mark's phone rang. It was still ringing a moment later as I passed by on the way to deliver his refreshments. No name or picture, just a number across the screen and above it in small letters was the word Sweden. He had the bathroom door pulled to and I realised he hadn't heard the phone. I assumed it must have been Grace calling. I was sure Mark had deleted her number from his phone hence why her name failed to come up. It couldn't have been the boys as they were in his contacts. It would be interesting to see if Mark let me know she had called. I didn't have to wait long. Not long after he got out of the bath, his phone rang again. This time he was there to check it.

'It's from Sweden 'he said as soon as he saw the screen.

'Well aren't you going to answer it then 'I questioned him as he dropped the phone back in the bowl.

'No I'm not, I don't know who it is.'

'I'll give you three guesses 'I said hardly containing my sarcasm.

'If it's not the boys I'm not interested.'

'Well, at least message them to make sure everything is okay.'

He assured me he would and I thought no more about it.

When I received an email from Grace later that same week regarding driving lessons for Alexander it confirmed it for me that it had been her calling. I assumed it was the usual case of her contacting Mark, him not responding, then Grace contacting me knowing I would deal with it.

From Grace
On Thu 13 Feb at 07.34

Hi Cleo, hope everything is splendid on this new decennium. Time for Alexander to go in to a more intense phase of driving.

He turns 18 in a couple of months, and needs to book his driving school soon to be able to get his driving license this spring (or summer) hopefully, so if it is possible for you to put money into his account this month it would be great.
If you or Mark have any questions don't hesitate to ask. I have a link to the driving school's prices but it is in Swedish though.

Cheers,
Grace

From Cleo
On Thu 13 Feb 2020 at 10.46

Hi Grace,
How are you? I'm happy to say this new decade has indeed got off to a splendid start, although I'm hoping there will be less surprises than in the last one! ;-)
Will transfer money either today or tomorrow. Both boys driving now! Scary how quickly time goes by.
Looking forward to seeing them both in May. We're thinking of going away for the weekend. Think it might be nice for them to have a change.
I hope you didn't mind me making travel plans with the boy's. I

know you said before, all arrangements must go through you but I figured they are old enough now to know what they're doing. Apologies if you feel differently.

Hope all's well with you,
Cleo x

From Grace
On Fri 14 2020 at 09.45

Hi Cleo and thank you!
We deserve the best of decades ▯
You can make any plans you want with them - I think it sounds great if you go on a trip, and you can communicate directly with them. (They are a bit confused about dates though so it might be that our plans collide at one point or the other ▯*).*
I will take them on a trip this fall - probably NY in late Sept or early Oct, or maybe Dec - to celebrate their 18 and 21st. But I will make sure that they know the dates when it is booked.
Happy Valentine's Day - I hope you get a great treat from dickhead ▯▯*and send him my love* ▯
Grace

From Cleo
On Fri 14 2020 at 11.41

Happy Valentines to you also!
It's fantastic having a partner who has been a complete and utter shit bag in a past life. They spend the rest of their future trying to make up for it ▯*. Flowers, chocolates, jewellery, meal out tonight. I will be sure to send your love as we toast to make him feel really guilty* ▯▯
Just transferred money but may take a few days as it's the

weekend.
I've just booked one trip so far. Boys coming over Friday 1st May for 3 nights. I've sent travel documents to Lucas. Will confirm with you dates for NY before booking anything else. Great choice for celebrating and partying (maybe why Mark chose to get married there second time round)!!

Have a good weekend and an amazing decade ?

Cleo x

Mark had indeed taken me out that night. We were feeling slightly worse for wear the next day and spent it lazing around doing as little as we could get away with. Mark snoozed on and off on the sofa whilst I channel hopped from the armchair unable to concentrate on one thing for too long. His mobile was on silent lying face up on the table next to me. As I reached for my glass of water which was standing not far from the phone I saw a call was coming through. It was the same number I had seen a few days ago. The last four digits had stuck in my mind -1966 - the year England won the world cup. This time though the word Sweden was missing. Did that mean the call was coming from somewhere in this country? I was puzzled. Had Grace come over to England? Although it was none of my business where Grace went I felt sure she would have contacted me in advance if she was coming over. Seconds later the number disappeared and the screen went black. As I sat wondering if she would call again the phone pinged with a notification. Without hesitation I picked up the phone, tapped in Marks ever so complicated password (my DOB) and opened up the text message.

Hey there! Eva here. Remember me? In London visiting my sister. Can we meet? Need to talk V. important. Back to Sweden Monday x

I thought the sound of my heart pumping out of my chest would wake Mark. I put my hand over my mouth to silence the words that were coming out. 'Not again, no, no, no 'I repeated over and over. Sick rose in my throat but I swallowed it back down, frozen to the armchair unable to make it to the toilet. I forced myself to take deep breaths and focus. Who the fuck was Eva? What did she need to speak to Mark about? Memories of searching for Grace on Facebook came flooding back. I would not go through that again. I couldn't if I wanted to. All I had was a first name and a phone number. Checking that Mark was in a deep sleep I got up and tiptoed to the kitchen, phone in hand. I took down Eva's number in my notebook before sending a text back to her from Mark's phone.

Hey. I remember you well. Can meet tomorrow. Where/when?

I prayed to Jesus and all the saints in heaven that she would get back quickly and thankfully my prayers were answered.

Duke of Sussex? For old times sake 12.00 x

Before giving myself a chance to think I typed back.

Ok

I got my phone and took photos of the texts then deleted the messages before going into the call log and deleting the phone call. I poured myself a glass of water and sipped from it as I reread the conversation. What the hell had I just done? I had made arrangements to meet with a woman called Eva tomorrow at midday in the Duke of Sussex. There were a couple of problems with my plan.

Firstly I had never seen Eva so I wouldn't know her if she was standing next to me.

Secondly I didn't know where the Duke of Sussex was let alone be there for 12.00.

With the sound of Mark's light snoring in the background I forced myself to concentrate and think logically. I had to meet her, of that there was no doubt. If Mark had been messing about with yet another woman I was going to get to the truth a lot bloody quicker than I did the last time. I wanted to hear it straight from the horses mouth. The words 'for old times sake 'reverberated in my head. How old was she talking about? Finding out where we were supposed to be meeting would be a step in the right direction at least. The Duke of Sussex had to be a pub.

I did the obvious and Goggled the name keeping the search to London. There were several as I expected. I narrowed my search to south west and west London. Mark disliked the north of the capital immensely and I knew he would not have been drinking in a boozer over that way. The results were way less. The next thing I typed into Goggle was 'Swedish communities in London'. I was banking on the fact that Eva's sister lived here. The search brought up four areas: Kensington, Hyde Park, Richmond and Chiswick. The Swedes certainly picked nice places to live. I cross referenced the name of the pub with each area and came up with one result. Chiswick. Only about four miles from Putney so that made sense. With nothing else to go on I would just have to trust my instinct which was telling me it was the right place. The next stumbling block was Eva's identity. I would have to cross that bridge when I came to it. I could not rely on the image of the stereotypical Swedish woman. I'd done that with Grace and she'd ended up looking the complete opposite. I would get to the pub an hour earlier than arranged and look out for a woman on her own arriving around midday. It would help enormously if she pulled up in a Volvo waving a Swedish flag wearing a t-shirt emblazoned with the words 'I LOVE ABBA on the back and 'MY NAME IS EVA 'across the front. Failing that I'd just to have to look like a complete weirdo and approach lone women asking them their name.

Fortunately for me Mark didn't take his phone off silent that day, barely looking at it. It was imperative that Eva did not have any contact with Mark for my plan to work. That night in bed as I lay staring up at the ceiling, sleep eluding me, a thought that had been just out of reach for most of the evening finally came within my minds grasp.

A tearful, angry conversation with Mark years ago during Gracegate. The exact words he used were a bit hazy in my memory but it was something along the lines of meeting a Swedish woman on a plane. Could Eva be that woman or were there plenty more where she came from? There was no point in speculating. I looked at the clock on the bedside table which read 02.18. If everything went according to plan within the next twelve hours all would be revealed.

We woke the next morning feeling the complete opposite of each other. Mark was refreshed and raring to go in the way most people are on the morning after the hangover day. I on the other hand was sleep deprived, nauseous and a bag of nerves at the thought of my meeting. I had to make an excuse to get away for a few hours which in itself was going to cause questions if not problems. It was an unwritten rule that if I was not working we always spent Sunday's together. If we weren't cooking a roast we would take a drive, looking for out of the way pubs serving Sunday lunch. Occasionally we would act like tourists and hit Greenwich or the Southbank, Columbia Road and Spitalfields Market. Of course it would have to be that Sunday that he suggested a trip to Covent Garden. I had to play it cool.

'I thought I told you 'I said looking at him as if he should know better. 'I'm meeting Lisa for lunch today. We arranged it ages ago. Patsy and Ron are looking after the kids to give her a break.'

'I honestly don't remember you saying that Cleo 'he said looking disappointed.

I refused to feel bad, silently reminding myself how many times he had lied to me in the past.

'That's a shame 'he continued. 'What time will you be back?'

'About three I should think 'I answered as casually as I could.

Then I realised the problem wasn't the time I was getting back, it was the time I was leaving. I'd estimated I would need to leave home before ten that morning to get to Chiswick, find a parking space and get plotted up somewhere that gave me the best vantage point.

As I got out of the shower Mark came into the bathroom and took the towel from me. He began drying my back lightly dabbing the material across my shoulder blades working his way down. I knew where this was leading and on any other day I would have been loving it. But today was different and I could not afford to be late. I hated rejecting his advances as he was always up for it if I came on to him. I could see the hurt in his eyes as I turned to him and told him I was in a rush and needed to do my hair.

'Bloody hell, what time are you leaving? 'he asked.

'About nine forty five 'I said.

'Surely you're going for breakfast, not lunch? 'he said

sarcastically.

'Actually, it's brunch and the quicker I get out of here the quicker I can get back to finish what we were just starting.'

He smiled at that and I kissed him on the lips giving his balls a little tickle to keep him going until I got home.

I got to Chiswick in record time. Light Sunday morning traffic meant my journey took half the time I expected it would.

The pub was situated on the corner of a road with Acton Common directly opposite. I parked the car easily and did a quick recce. The pub only had one entrance which was helpful. There was a bench on the edge of the common that I could sit on with a clear view of the door. One hour and forty minutes to go. I put my AirPods in and listened to my audible book. I gave up on that, unable to concentrate on the words coming through my eardrums. I played scrabble with a friend, checked my emails and browsed through some photos. In the end I settled on listening to my playlist.

Just as I was humming along to The Waterboys singing 'The Whole Of The Moon 'I spotted a woman on my side of the road walking towards the zebra crossing. I checked the time. It was ten to twelve. Her mid length hair was a dirty blonde, parted in the middle and cut into a sharp bob. Shorter than me and somewhat heavier, the clothes she wore suited her frame perfectly. A navy ribbed puffa jacket nipped in at the waist. Dark blue jeans with Timberland style boots. A patterned scarf covered her chin and huge sunglasses covered her eyes and half her forehead although I could still see she had a nice profile. Perfect attire for the day which was cold with a bright sun overhead. My eyes hidden under my own sunglasses never left her and as she walked past me, then stopped, waiting to cross the road I saw the messenger bag she was wearing. Attached to the strap where it joined the bag was a giant leather tassel with a shiny letter E hanging off of it.

Twenty-eight

I knew without a shadow of a doubt it was her. Just as a car was slowing down to allow her to cross over I threw caution to the wind and shouted out 'Eva'. The woman swung her head round to the sound of her name and pushed her sunglasses up on her head. I did the same and our eyes met. Complete puzzlement from Eva which was only to be expected. An attempt at a friendly smile from me. She stepped back from the kerb as I walked towards her.

'You've come to meet Mark, right?'

'Sorry 'she said frown lines appearing on her forehead 'but who are you and where's Mark?'

'I'm his partner and Mark is at home with no idea that you're here.'

'But 'she faltered. 'He sent me a text last night. We arranged to meet today.'

I explained it was me who had intercepted the text message and replied to it. How I had put my detective hat on to locate her. How I had assumed they were having a relationship or had been in one in recent years and I was there to find out if my assumptions had been correct. Without wanting to sound mean spirited I pointed out that even if Mark had read the text he wouldn't have got back to her.

'It was you wasn't it 'I said 'calling from Sweden earlier in the week. Mark was never going to answer your calls.'

She was weighing me up, deciding which way to play the situation. She was either going to tell all or piss off. I had to persuade her to take the first option.

'I apologise for deceiving you but it was the only way I could think of to speak to you 'I said trying to sound sincere.

'But why do you want to speak to me? 'she asked.

I couldn't stand it any longer. I had been working myself

up since reading the text message on Mark's phone, imagining all sorts of scenarios. The thought that scared me the most was knowing that if he had cheated on me, this time it would have to be the end of us. If he was looking for something more than the totally fulfilling relationship we had already, I was on a hiding to nothing.

'Please 'I begged, 'just tell me and put me out of my misery. Are you having an affair with Mark?'

Eva reached out and took both my hands in hers. She spoke softly, with only a trace of an accent.

'I haven't seen or heard from Mark in twenty years. The last time I saw him was over there' she said, pointing to the pub across the road. 'It's where we used to meet when I was over from Sweden visiting my sister and her family.'

The relief that flooded through my veins left me weak and I staggered backwards to sit down. I let out a huge sigh and slumped forward on the bench, head down trying to process my emotions. Gratitude that Mark wasn't having an affair. Bewildered as to why she would contact him after so long. Anticipation about what I was going to hear next. I sat up and told myself to get a grip.

Eva sat next to me at a slight angle so she could look at me as she spoke.

'I thought there was a good chance that Mark might ignore me and I made my mind up that if he did I would forget about it and never contact him again. I never imagined his girlfriend would turn up and now I'm in a dilemma. Do I tell you what I came to tell him or do I walk away?'

'Tell me 'I said. 'I'm a great listener and now I know I hadn't even met him when you were together, whatever you have to say won't affect me in the slightest.'

She was quiet for a minute or so, lost in thought.

'I've just realised 'she said with a laugh, 'I don't even know your name.'

'Cleo 'I answered smiling at her and holding out my hand.

She shook it firmly and asked if I would like to join her in a glass of wine.

'Does the pope pray? 'I joked as we made our way towards the place where she used to meet the man who would eventually become the love of my life.

Once settled in a cosy corner of the pub, two large glasses of Malbec and a bag of cashew nuts on the table between us she told me what she came to tell my partner.

'I have to go back a long way before Mark was ever in the picture. I won't bore you with too many details but you'll see in the end why it's relevant.'

'Fire away, I've got all day 'I said taking a sip of wine. I loved a good story and I had a feeling I was going to hear one.

She had fallen in love and lust with a Spanish guy she had met in a bar in Stockholm one night in 1989. Eva was there winding down with work colleagues, whilst Luis, a pharmaceutical salesman from Barcelona was relaxing with a beer following the most boring two day conference he had ever attended. Eva had gone to the bar to get the drinks in, started chatting to Luis and never made it back to her colleagues. She left them gasping for their drinks while she was swept off her feet by "The most beautiful man I had ever seen". Within months Eva had said her goodbyes to family and friends and relocated to Barcelona to be with him.

Sunk back in the armchair taking occasional sips from my glass I was enjoying this. Girl meets boy. Girl gets boy. Girl moves to be with boy.

Five years into their relationship when Eva was twenty six and Luis was thirty two they decided the spare room in their flat would be put to better use as a nursery and set about making a baby to put in it. Two years later with the spare room still empty they made an appointment to see a fertility specialist. After extensive tests on both of them the blame was laid at Eva's feet, or rather her womb. A womb that did not appear to be behaving as it should. The doctor explained that it wasn't out of the question for Eva to fall pregnant, she just might need a bit of help. As soon as IVF was mentioned she switched off. She was pragmatic and accepted that some things were just not meant to be. Luis on the other hand refused to accept the news as casually and made no secret of the fact that he wanted a big family, three, possibly four kids. They kept making love and she kept getting her period. The disappointment took it's toll and after nearly five years of trying they decided it best to go their separate ways before resentment for each other set in. At the end of 1998 Eva moved out of the flat they shared and decided to go back home to Stockholm. She never stopped thinking about Luis, not for a moment and it was hell resisting the urge to call him every time she picked up her phone. But resist she did and as the weeks passed she even managed to enjoy the company of other men, Mark being one of them. She was indeed the woman Mark had mentioned who had sat next to him on a plane departing from Stockholm, bound for London. They started chatting before the plane took off and were still deep in conversation when they touched down on the tarmac at Heathrow. Mark had told her he was returning from a stag do. She was making a trip to see her sister who lived in Chiswick. She could not remember which one of them made the suggestion to have a drink in one of the airport hotel bars as they disembarked (I'd bet my life it was Mark who came up with that idea). What she did remember was having great sex in the hotel room that they booked for the night. In the morning they exchanged numbers and both parties agreed it would be nice to do it again sometime. Uncomplicated sex with no ties or commitments was exactly what she needed to get over her lost love, Luis.

'We met another four or five times during that year. I would let him know I was coming over and he would book us a room in a small hotel he knew in Hammersmith. We would meet in the Duke for a couple of drinks, go to the hotel for the night, have sex and kiss goodbye in the morning.'

As much as I was enjoying her recollections of times gone by I was itching to know why she had contacted Mark after so many years and what was the very important talk she wanted to have with him.

She continued, telling me how meeting Mark had been fun and their tryst's had kept her mind off her Spanish amor for short periods. However the thought of having to live the rest of her days without Luis was unbearable. In November of 1999 in the very pub we were sharing a drink in, she finished the 'arrangement 'with Mark, telling him honestly that he had helped her see what it was she really wanted and thanked him for the great sex. He thanked her back and wished her well, never expecting to hear from her ever again. By then Eva hadn't spoken to Luis for nearly a year but when she called him and he answered with 'Where are you my sweetheart? 'she knew he still loved her. Their reunion when she returned to Barcelona confirmed that he was the only man for her and she promised him she would undergo IVF in the hope they could complete the family they had always wanted.

Up until that moment her dialogue had been steady and articulate but at the mention of Luis and IVF she crumbled and tears threatened to fall. I thought it best to keep quiet. I had only met the woman an hour before and had no idea what it took to console her.

'Listen to me 'she said, wiping her eyes. 'I'm so sorry, you've not got a word in since I started. Please tell me a little about yourself.'

I had already decided I wasn't giving much away. I was keeping to the bare minimum until I discovered what her agenda was. I wanted to know what Mark had told her although I had a rough idea that it would have been as far from the truth as China was to South America. I was in the mood for asking not telling.

'What did Mark tell you about himself when you met him?' I asked.

'Not a lot, apart from the fact he had a son from his first marriage, that he was single and not interested in a serious relationship.'

That was all I needed to know. As expected Mark had not mentioned the fact that he had a wife in London and a mistress in Sweden who had given birth to Lucas during the time Eva and Mark were seeing each other. I went on to tell a very evasive version of how we met eighteen years ago, making it sound like the most innocent of beginnings.

I was more interested in her side of the story and asked her if she had gone ahead with the IVF after her reunion with Luis.

'I fully intended to. Two weeks after we got back together we made an appointment at a fertility clinic. In the days leading up to the appointment I was waking up every morning feeling so sick. The sickness lasted all day and into the night. It was difficult to keep food down and I began to worry there was something seriously wrong with me. I went to see my doctor who gave me a full examination. He was aware of my malfunctioning womb and even though it was highly unlikely, he wanted to do a test to rule out any chance I could be pregnant.'

I picked up my glass, taking a slug rather than a sip as I braced myself for what was coming next even though it was pretty obvious.

Eva looked at me with an expression on her face that read 'you know what's coming don't you'.

'How pregnant were you? 'I asked.

'Two days later after keeping the fact that I was pregnant from Luis I had a scan that confirmed I was three months pregnant. I was in complete shock. My options were grim. Terminate the pregnancy without telling Luis. Tell Luis another man's sperm had been more compatible with my eggs and succeeded where he had failed and then terminate the pregnancy.'

'I'm going to get us another drink 'I said as I got up and made my way to the bar. As I passed the window I saw my car and knew that would be staying there till the morning. This was not the time for soft drinks. I would call a cab to take me home.

In the end she chose none of her original options. She told Luis she was pregnant by another man and after his initial shock he asked her if she would consider keeping the baby so they could raise it as their own. He was a Catholic and had very strong views regarding abortion. If she went ahead with the pregnancy she wanted everyone to think it was Luis's baby. If anyone questioned the due date of their new addition they would tell people how they had met one night to discuss getting back with each other and how one thing lead to another. Eva said she was in awe of the way Luis handled the situation. She expected some resentment towards her during the pregnancy and fretted that he would not bond with the baby when it arrived. She needn't have worried. He told her he loved her more than ever and kissed her ever expanding belly every day speaking Spanish to the miracle growing inside her.

'Weren't you worried what the baby would look like? 'I asked.

'Not at all. I think the reason I was attracted to Mark in the first place was because he reminded me so much of Luis. Both of them were dark haired with brown eyes and olive skin. I really only went for one type of man back then. Tall dark and handsome 'she said with a smile.

They got married in March 2000 and Eva gave birth to a 8lb 9oz baby girl two months later.

I had no idea why the sex of Eva's baby made such a difference to my reaction but it did.

Mark could have a daughter.

A twenty year old daughter living in Spain.

I could not imagine what a daughter of Mark would look like. I knew three of his sons and I was hard pushed to see a resemblance in any of them to their father. Was she dark like her potential father or blonde like her mother?

Eva took her phone from her bag and after scrolling through it she slid it across the table to me.

'That's Sofia.'

She was stunning. Now, I know in this day and age, we can all look amazing on a mobile phone if we apply enough filters. My girlfriends had taken pictures of me on holiday following a crazy night out. After the filters were applied I could have been mistaken for Cindy Crawford circa 1996. In reality I looked more like Bridget Bardot circa 2016 - download the right apps and suddenly everyone's a supermodel. Sofia was unfiltered, a perfect combination of facial features. She had her mum's blue eyes which was very fortunate. If Mark was her father she was lucky not to have inherited his eyes which were a nice colour but slitty and small. She had a lovely shaped mouth with a natural pout and a strong jawline similar to Mark's it had to be said.

'She's beautiful 'I said passing the phone back.

I had a question for Eva and I had to ask it in a sensitive way.

'Was Mark the only man you were sleeping with? '(Not sure I achieved my goal on the sensitivity front).

'No, he wasn't. There were others during that period.'

I was surprised at her answer.

'So how can you be so sure Sofia is Mark's? 'I asked.

'Well, I can't be sure. I worked out the dates and who I slept with and Mark seemed to be the obvious candidate.'

I looked at her doubtfully, feeling my hackles rise ever so slightly.

'She looks like him 'Eva continued with a shrug of her shoulders.

That wasn't enough proof for me. As Eva herself had pointed out only minutes before, she only had one type. Tall dark and handsome. The majority of good looking men have strong jaw lines and plump lips. Sofia could have inherited her beauty from any one of Eva's one night stands.

I shook my head letting her know I wasn't happy with her weak reasoning.

'You can't just go round accusing men of fathering children without strong evidence. What does your husband have to say about this? 'I asked.

'Luis and I only ever discussed the fact that he wasn't her biological father once. I thought it only right that she should know the truth but Luis strongly disagreed. I asked would he at least consider telling Sofia when she was twenty-one.'

I did a quick calculation in my head.

'She's not twenty-one till next year, so why now? 'I asked, totally unprepared for the tragic answer she gave me.

'Luis died from a sudden brain haemorrhage six months ago 'she said, her eyes filling with tears as she spoke. She pulled a tissue from her pocket and continued.

'Sofia is beyond devastated. Her and Luis adored each other and I seem to be a poor consolation prize at the moment. I'm struggling with my own grief. He was the love of my life. I don't know how to help myself, so how can I help my daughter?'

By now the tears were falling freely. I went to her side of the table and crouched down putting my arms round her. I told her to let it all out. She was a quiet crier unlike me who snivelled and hiccuped and let everyone within a two mile radius know that I was unhappy.

Eventually her tears subsided and I went back to my chair. We were both emotionally exhausted.

I asked her if she was still in contact with any of the men she had slept with during that time. When she said she was in contact with two of them I asked why she had approached

Mark first and not the others.

'I wanted Mark to be Sofia's dad.'

As cruel at it seemed I had no choice than to be honest with Eva. If, (a one in three chance IF) Mark did happen to be the father I needed to let her know that his reaction to the news would be far from joyful. If she was expecting him to jump on a flight to Spain to meet his daughter she had a rude awakening.

'Have you seriously thought this through?'

Not giving her a chance to answer, I continued. 'No other man will be a substitute for Luis. Sofia should be left alone to grieve for the man that she believed to be her father. I promise you Eva, nothing good can come of this.'

We spent the rest of the afternoon discussing the pros and cons of keeping secrets and the consequences that followed. She sobbed again as she showed me pictures of Sofia with Luis. She was right about Luis and Mark looking similar though. They could have been brothers.

By five o'clock Eva had come to the conclusion that it was in everyone's best interests to keep shtum about the unknown identity of her daughters father.

We parted on the street with wine breath kisses and strong hugs making each other drunken promises to 'be there if you ever need me'.

She took my number but I knew I would never see or hear from her again.

Twenty-nine

I put the thought of Eva and Sofia to the back of my mind but somehow they just kept worming their way to the front of it. How I wished I could take a leaf out of Mark's book and completely switch off from unwanted thoughts. I thought of Eva unable to comfort her daughter, both women caught up in their own grief. How would Sofia feel knowing the man she loved and adored wasn't her flesh and blood. Would it enhance her life in anyway to know that her biological father was either a man who had met up with her mum for sex in a hotel room a handful of times or a one night stand?

I thought back to the relationship I had with my own mother and how much I had adored her. If I, after her death, was informed that I actually was adopted and we were unrelated I would have been truly devastated. Then I thought about the part I had played in all this. I had persuaded Eva not to confront Mark. She was grieving and vulnerable and so wanted to do the right thing by her daughter. I could have just as easily swayed her the other way and convinced her it would be in everyone's best interests to talk to him about it, to gauge his reaction.

Who did I think I was to deny Mark knowledge of a potential daughter?

I was going round and round in circles unsure whether I had made the right decision or not. Then there was Mark's boys to consider. What if I was denying them a sister? Elaine and Paul, a granddaughter? John and Kerry a niece and their boys a cousin? The only consolation was the Palmer family were not close, in fact rather splintered. I needn't waste my time worrying that Sofia was missing out on a whole lot of warmth and love. We weren't dealing with The Brady bunch.

When I started having trouble sleeping at night I knew I

would have to take action.

Unable to talk to anyone about my thoughts I started to write them down. Was there a reason Mark had such an issue with responsibility especially when it came to his offspring, or his relationship's with women?

Of course there was. No need to consult with Freud on that one. We are all, every single one of us, in part the results of our upbringing. Nature does have a part to play but it's the interaction between nature and nurture that can make or break mind and spirit. If a child is born with learning difficulties to parents with a negative attitude, who insist their child is incapable of this or unable to do that it will hold the child back. Their full potential will not be achieved. The same goes for some physical disabilities. Ask any athlete who has ever competed in the paralympics and I bet most of them will tell you they had positive role models as a child. I think Mark was a difficult troublesome child with issues that could have been sorted out or at least talked about before he reached manhood. Having said that, whatever has gone before has made him the man I love today. It's not despite his shortcomings that I love him, it is because of them. At the end of the day, apart from it getting dark, there's not really a lot you can do about damage done in our early years. Therapists who charge ninety pound an hour will tell you different. Best selling books from psychologists with titles such as "60 days to forget your childhood " will tell you different. There's a lot of harping on nowadays from people who want to blame someone else for their miserable lives. Sometimes it just boils down to the simple fact that you just have to get on with it. Mark is very good at that. In his words 'Shit happens and you move on'.

I was very happy with my childhood, it was only when I met Mark that my life went to pot. But it was my choice to stay and I'm not ashamed to say that the turbulent relationship that we had actually suited me at times. I could be accused of having a couple of wires loose in my brain and I wouldn't disagree with that. At times I enjoyed the rows and fights I had with Mark. The energy it took, the high it gave me, the calmness of the come down and the making up. I am absolutely not advocating violence in any relationship if there is fear involved. My heart goes out to people who are trapped in violent relationships who are scared to speak for fear of getting a slap. I was never frightened of Mark. I sometimes pushed him to his limits to see if he could scare me but he rarely did. I don't do that anymore and neither should I have done it in the first place.

I cast my mind back to when Mark and I first met and wrote down my thoughts starting from there. It's incredible how much you can remember when you put your mind to it, although some of it I'd much rather forget. My thoughts kept coming, turning the words into chapters and before I knew it I was writing a book. Unburdening my mind during the day allowed me to sleep through the night again.

I was looking forward to continuing with my writing on our holiday in Mexico. I had visions of me relaxing in the shade with a large margarita by my side tapping away on the iPad to my hearts content. Then Corona virus hit town and put paid to that. Having our holiday cancelled was a drop in the ocean compared to what was going on elsewhere in the world. After Boris Johnson announced the country was going into lock down I had ample opportunity to dedicate time to my writing. Then I thought to myself - who am I kidding? Write a book, I don't even know where to insert speech marks or how to use capital letters. I typed on regardless hoping that a You Tube tutorial in formatting a manuscript may help.

Seeing my thoughts on the screen before me or scribbled in notebooks dotted all over the house helped enormously and I would advise anyone with problems that need sorting to write them down or type them out. Failing that, drive out to the country, find a massive field and scream your head off. Anything that gets it out of your system.

My book was taking shape but I really wasn't sure what to do with it. I browsed the internet for information on self publishing. Oh, how easy it all sounded until I downloaded the apps and wondered if I'd changed my computer setting to Mandarin. Having waited till 2015 to step into the twenty first century with my mobile that I still have trouble mastering I was hardly going to be able to produce a book.

It was around that time that I discovered I had a guardian angel. She came not in the form of a celestial being looking down from heaven but a woman from Sweden who had been in my life one way or another for the past six years. In May I happened to mention to Grace in one of my emails regarding the boys that I was writing a book and asked her if she would be interested in reading it. She was a big part of it and I wanted her opinion. She was enthusiastic and encouraging and understood my pain regarding self publishing even though she is a whizz on the computer and has self published three books herself. I very cheekily put it to her that maybe she could help me. She kindly agreed and somehow without too much effort on my part, Grace has gone from reading it to editing it. If you are reading this, she's only gone and done the treble and published it for me as well.

Epilogue

AUGUST 2020

I was wrong about never hearing from Eva again. She sent me a text this morning, that I read in Starbucks whilst waiting in the queue for my large salted caramel, extra shot, extra hot latte.

Hey Cleo, wanted to let you know. I've managed to contact the two men who apart from Mark could potentially be Sofia's father. They have both agreed to take a DNA test. If there is no match then Mark is her father. I'll let you know the results as soon as I receive them. Until then x

ACKNOWLEDGEMENTS

MY MOTHER - My heroine

Growing up, you taught me to always try and see the good in people. That's easier said than done Mum. Some people just haven't got a lot of good in them. Even you would have struggled with Mark at the beginning.
I know if you had lived you would have tried unsuccessfully to talk me out of my relationship with him. I hope you are looking down on us now appreciating how much he has changed and how happy he makes me. I think of you often, how you would approach strangers in the street admiring a bag they were carrying or an unusual pair of shoes they were wearing. Standing in a queue you thought nothing of tapping on the shoulder of the lady in front telling her what an amazing head of hair she had. You knew that an unexpected compliment could make someone's day.

What about the afternoon we spent at Battersea Dogs Home when I was about ten years of age. We were looking for a puppy. How we ended up with an eight year old Labrador with three legs, one eye and several bald patches is beyond me. You said he was the most beautiful dog in the world. When I asked what was so beautiful about him you stroked his floppy ears and told me to feel how incredibly soft they were. I'll never be as kind as you but I am as strong and for that I'm truly grateful.

GRACE - My Scandinavian pen pal
(she's a quarter Norwegian)

At times I feel I know you so well, then at times like I don't know you at all. I lack the basic's - Do you have brothers or sisters? Are you a vegetarian? How do you take your coffee? What job do you do? Are you in a relationship? Your feelings on Donald Trump?
What I do know for sure is that you are kind and forgiving. I know that you have made me laugh out loud and cry hysterically over the past six years with your revelations, accusations and protestations. I admire your refusal to fade into the background and to bounce back with such spirit from a very painful experience.
There is a bottle of champagne somewhere out there with our names on it. I look forward to much merriment when it is opened and we clink glasses to toast two of the strongest women ever.

LUCAS & ALEXANDER - My stepsons ;-)
What lucky boys you are to have such a loving and well adjusted mother. From what I have seen she has brought you up to be the best versions of yourself. You are also lucky to have the love of your dad. Believe me it worked out better for you both in the long run that he wasn't around so much when you were growing up. Hopefully you got to see the best of him. You are growing into fine young men and your dad is proud of you. Quite rightly he doesn't take any credit for how you've turned out. It goes to your mum who deserves it all. Bear that in mind when she asks you to help out around the house or do some cooking! Try very hard to take after her and carefully cherry-pick parts of your father to emulate. Enjoy the wonderful and exciting lives ahead of you and remember if you ever come across a beautiful Spanish girl with the bluest of eyes and olive skin with hair the colour of your dad's when he was young don't fall in love with her. She

may be your sister.

EVA - The one that got away
Just when I thought there was nothing left to reveal about Mark, you came along to prove me wrong. Even if you do find out the true identity of Sofia's father don't tell her. Always let her think that she belongs to you and Luis. No deathbed confessions when you're an old woman and on your way to meet your maker. A not so wise old woman once told me 'What you don't know won't hurt you'. I've often disagreed with that saying but in this case I'd take that advice if I were you.

MARK - The breaker of my heart
So it appears we're deliriously happily stuck with each other. No matter how hard we've tried over the years we just won't let go will we? My broken heart has healed with virtually no scars and I'm giving you full responsibility to keep it out of harms way. I'm not sorry to deny you the fact that you may have a daughter and if you ever find out and don't agree with my actions, then forgive me. I've had to forgive you far worse. We started our relationship with you as the keeper of Swedish secrets. Now it seems I may have one of my very own.

Printed in Great Britain
by Amazon

37597720R00165